To Pa
Ma

Our great
trip July 21

CHALLENGING WATERS

X
Dad.

CHALLENGING WATERS

The Diary of a
Lake District Swimmer

Written and Illustrated

By

J.C.Mather

SUBLIME SWIMMING PRESS

DEDICATION

This book is dedicated to my late parents, John and Margaret.

Copyright © John Mather, 2018

Published by Sublime Swimming Press 2018

British Library Cataloguing-in-Publication data
A catalogue record for this book is available from the British Library

ISBN 978-0-9955990-0-0

Printed and bound by Jellyfish Solutions

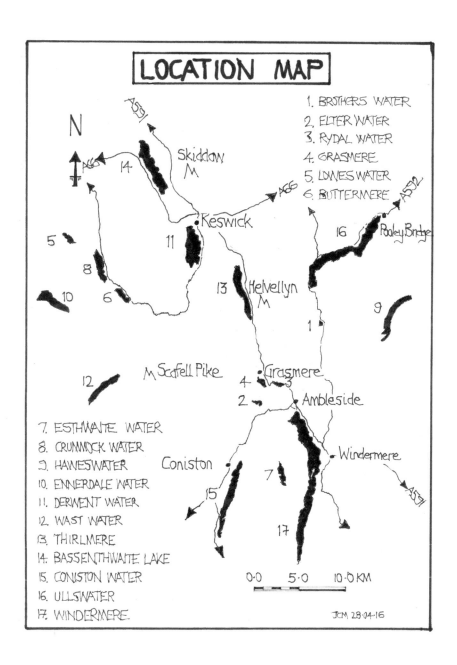

LOCATION MAP

N

1. BROTHERS WATER
2. ELTER WATER
3. RYDAL WATER
4. GRASMERE
5. LOWES WATER
6. BUTTERMERE

A591

A66

Skiddaw M

14

A66

Keswick

5

8

10

6

11

13

Helvellyn M

16

Pooley Bridge

A592

9

1

M Scafell Pike

12

Grasmere

4

2

Ambleside

7. ESTHWAITE WATER
8. CRUMMOCK WATER
9. HAWESWATER
10. ENNERDALE WATER
11. DERWENT WATER
12. WAST WATER
13. THIRLMERE
14. BASSENTHWAITE LAKE
15. CONISTON WATER
16. ULLSWATER
17. WINDERMERE

Coniston

Windermere

A591

15

7

17

0·0   5·0   10·0 KM

JCM 28·04·16

DISCLAIMER

The views expressed in the book are those of the author alone and do not necessarily reflect the views or opinions of any body or organisation representing, promoting or involved in the management of the Lake District.

Equally, the author cannot be held responsible or accountable for the actions or opinions expressed by any member of the public or organisation considering or being involved in open water swimming.

CONTENTS

*"….Only those who will risk going too far can possibly
find out how far one can go…"*

T.S.Eliot (1888–1965)

ACKNOWLEDGEMENTS

I am certain that my project would never even have got off the ground had it not been for the kindness and generosity of so many people who gave their time and knowledge so freely. It has been an honour to receive such friendship and goodwill and I have attempted to list everyone, as well as every organisation, that has contributed in the following page, titled "Helpers and Supporters".

I am indebted to Anna Goddard and the team at Carnegie Book Production as well as Robert Mather; Karin Crofts at the West Cumbria Rivers Trust, Tim Duckmanton at the Lake District National Park Authority; Jim Wood and Malcolm Sutherland for reviewing and contributing to the original text.

I must extend special thanks to Keswick Launch Company, Windermere Outdoors Adventure Centre and Speedo UK for their particular generosity. I wish to make particular mention of Cumbrian Newspapers and BBC Radio Cumbria for their support and coverage.

So many have encouraged and offered unstinting belief in my journey; and I must cite Stephen and Caroline White of Carlisle Library; my colleagues in the Capita Building, Carlisle; Beth and Louise.

Last and by no means least I am eternally grateful to Robert, Annette, Laura and Robbie for their countless cups of teas and biscuits and their many suggestions, as well as checking and re-correcting my text and supporting my swims by rowing alongside me. If only I could spell as well as I swim.....

HELPERS AND SUPPORTERS
(Listed in order of appearance)

Swimmers
Tom Baker, Paul Ryan, James Slater, Adam Crawford, Laura Mather, Kevin Hull, Jordan Hull, Matt Pearson, Ben Purdham and Samantha Wilson

Canoeists
Mike Pinske, Paul Butterworth, Andy Sims and Caroline Preston

Boat Crews
David Cathcart, Martin Penny, Craig Irving, Annette Mather, Laura Mather, Robbie Mather, David Barrett and Josh Barre

Supporters
David Cathcart, David Barrett, Martin Penny, Robert Mather, Annette Mather, Susan Hull, Jonathan Sander and Graham Dallas

Wigton Baths Trust
Alan Pitcher, Michael Bryceson, Mave Tyas, Dawn Allen, Robin & Anna Swindells and James Foley

Swim Coaching
Joe Smith, Norman Trusty and Faye Carruthers

Windermere Route Planning
Thomas G. Noblett and John McAllister

Swimming Organisations
"Swim the Lakes", "Epic Events" and "Chillswim"

Boat Hire, Launch Facilities and Permits
National Trust, United Utilities, Keswick Launch Company, "Platty Plus" Water Sports Centre, St. Patrick's Boat Landing, Windermere Outdoors Adventure Centre and Bowness Bay Marina

Nutritional Advice
Science in Sports

Swimming Equipment
Speedo UK

FOREWORD

In 2014, I decided to celebrate my 60th birthday by attempting to swim the length of all 17 lakes contained within the English Lake District, little realising the time, effort or the planning that would be involved.

These 17 "lakes", and that's what I'm intending to describe this diverse collection of so called meres, waters and one solitary lake, range in size from Brotherswater, the smallest which is just under a half a mile in length, to Windermere, the longest natural lake in England, which comes in at a whopping ten and a half miles long.

All 17 lakes have one thing in common, being relatively low lying and readily accessible from the road network, so provide a safety outlet if things, heaven forbid, go wrong. The challenge does not include upland tarns or those waters that could be classified as lakes but are located "in the fells".

I have been very lucky that friends have been only too keen to swim alongside, others even offered to canoe in support without any persuasion, let alone having to resort to arm twisting! And I've estimated that I will have to swim a total distance of 40 miles, which is far greater than that covered by someone attempting to cross the English Channel, to achieve this task.

It is remarkable how popular open water swimming is becoming in the Lake District. Its phenomenal growth in the last few years must be the result of several providential factors, including well publicised swimming events like the Great North Swim which is held in Windermere annually and Great Britain's successes in open swimming and triathlons on the world stage.

Even so, I have been surprised to discover some failings with water quality in some of the lakes and I hope that my book might, in some small way, encourage the authorities and powers-to-be to address matters. Regrettably, I also discover that I am not allowed to swim in four of the lakes, for one reason or other, but all will be explained.

I have decided to write an account of my journey for four reasons: to celebrate all the good people I have met and marvellous adventures that I have undertaken; to highlight the beauty and fragility of this wonderful land; to draw attention to some failings in water quality, pollution and wanton vandalism I have encountered; and to encourage other swimmers to try swimming in the lakes.

I must stress the importance of everyone's responsibility for the care and upkeep of the lakes. After all, the Lake District National Park, which has now been awarded World Heritage Status by UNESCO and attracts more than 16 million visitors a year, is located in a region of outstanding natural beauty. The lakes were formed by glaciation more than 15,000 years ago and their surprising diversity in size and ecology makes them an invaluable asset to the County of Cumbria. As well as containing England's longest natural lake, the National Park also possesses England's highest mountain, Scafell Pike, which is 3,209ft high.

And finally, but by no means least, I must stress to anyone considering venturing into open waters to remember the one absolute, cardinal rule of swimming: safety is paramount!

INTRODUCTION

I've always had a passion for outdoor swimming. Perhaps it's in my genes? After all, my grandad inspired me with his tales of swimming exploits prior to the First World War in Bury's reservoirs and the town's Victorian baths, a spectacular and long demolished municipal edifice, in what I now realise is in the heartland of industrial Lancashire.

I spent my formative years braving the best of what Greater Manchester's public swimming pools could offer, before moving to Cumbria in my early 20s and developing a passion for outdoor swimming. The bug started with tarn swims in the Lake District and snorkelling in Scotland with the local sub-aqua club in a hand-made wet suit. Many of my best adventures seemed to involve climbing to remote mountain tarns or braving gushing rivers, including desperate exploits long before the expression "wild swimming" had been invented or the craze became popular. Back then, it was a wonder if I encountered a fellow "tarn bagger" on the fells, let alone anything other than disapproving smirks from groups of passing ramblers.

I have always preferred to swim breaststroke, out of choice, and can never profess to be a "speed merchant". Nevertheless, I am extremely proud of my past swimming exploits, undertaken on various swimming expeditions and adventures involving rivers, lakes and seas at home and abroad. They have all provided some wonderful opportunities to enjoy great scenery and meet some truly inspiring characters.

And it has no doubt helped that I have been so conditioned to cold water swimming "over the years" that it has almost become second nature. After all, I learned to swim my first lengths in a remote moorland pool at an early age where the water was freezing, absolutely freezing.

Facilities of this small pool, situated in the remote moorland village of Egerton, near Bolton, were spartan, to say the least. Nevertheless, I would not miss Mary Pennycook's Saturday morning learners' class for anything in the world. Her enthusiasm conquered my fear and taught me to swim well.

She was that rare species of dedicated teacher; patient, caring and thorough. It was a joy to attend her classes and be inspired by my fellow swimmers. She lived for swimming and wanted to pass on her love of swimming to as many others as best she could.

We travelled every Saturday morning the eight or so miles to the Baths in her old three wheeled Reliant Robin, come road-works, hail, sleet, snow or ice. And believe me: some of those winter trips were particularly fraught.

The car's name of "Reliant" was particularly inappropriate as I am convinced that Hell has no fury like a Reliant Robin forced to start in the dead of winter. Sometimes the snow was so thick on the ground that I had to help push the car up the inclined frozen cobbled surface connecting her house to the main road. Desperately it would slide and slither, frantic for purchase. Occasionally, my efforts were to no avail, and anyway the combined noise of racing engine and screeching tyres was usually sufficient to summon neighbours from the adjoining row of stone cottages to leave their breakfast table and lend a hand and help shovel out snow.

We always seemed to just about make it to Egerton and swim: even that time when the water temperature barely rose above 55 degrees Fahrenheit. Now, that was cold, believe me! Well, we had started, hadn't we? So, surely we might as well continue. Well, that was me and a meagre handful of similarly single minded learners. We weren't going to be put off by a wee touch of hypothermia, now were we?

Anyway I survived; and as they say if it doesn't kill you, it will make you stronger....

I eventually progressed to swimming abroad. And that created even greater challenges and more splendid experiences. Not all my swims have gone to plan, far from it, and I know only too well how important it is to prepare for the unexpected. Consider the time that I thought that I was going to be arrested by the Turkish Navy whilst swimming down the mile wide Bosphorus in the shadow of the Gallipoli peninsula. And this was despite all the necessary documents being "in place".

I don't know what was worse: nearly being run down by a coastguard patrol boat in the ensuing melee; or, listening to my companion as she announced, excitedly, that "The captain waved at me!"

Another time, I travelled all the way to Hungary with the intention of taking part in an annual crossing of the width of the majestic Lake Balaton only to find that organisers had decided to postpone the race until a later date in the year because they deemed the water was too cold....

Too cold, I ask you? I wish that the same organisers had been persuaded to join me in an early morning dip in Siberia's Lake Baikal in water barely registering a bone chilling 5 degrees Centigrade. Now, that was cold.

There have been some memorable moments and exceptional highlights, not least crossing the fearsome mile wide Corryvreckan whirlpool off Scotland's Isle of Jura. This was undertaken as part of an exhausting week-long camping and swimming trip around the Western Isles, in Scotland, organised by "Swim Trek". And the less said about those blessed midges the better.

Fortunately, swims in Jordan's portion of the Dead Sea and Iceland's many splendid open air pools proved to be much more leisurely affairs. No matter, taking part in the inaugural "Great North Swim" held in Windermere in September 2008 made me realise how superb swimming in the English Lake District can be.

There is definitely no room for complacency. And the maxim that comedians and boxers are only as good as their last "gig" applies equally to any swimmer who is permanently striving to challenge their own swimming capabilities, be it in terms of colder water or extended durations.

It makes good sense. After all, one of my canoeing colleagues is wont to quote his time honoured maxim: "Life's not a rehearsal". Why settle for blandness or second best, I ask you?

I fully realise the need to prepare, rigorously, for my Lake District challenge and I have tried to "cover all posts" by a combination of regular distance training in my local pool in Carlisle; attending a refresher course in open water swimming and, last but by no means least, seeking advice from two former Channel swimmers. And, surely, advice can't get any better than that!

MIND OVER MATTER

Thursday 20 February 2014

It has been an absolute privilege to have made the acquaintance of so many really helpful and inspirational swimmers as a result of my previous endeavours in water.

Take my invitation to meet former Channel Swimmers, Joseph "Joe" Smith and Norman Trusty, "…whenever I am in Dover…", for example. It's a timely opportunity to hear of their past glories and gain some advice for my impending challenge.

Visitors to Dover can't fail to grasp the town's crucial role in Channel Swimming over the last 140 or so years, ever since Captain Webb became the first person to successfully swim the Channel in 1875. And Joe and Norman volunteer one day a week in Dover Museum cataloguing its vast collection of records connected with Channel Swimming. Both are well qualified to carry out this role and are both past inductees of the international Marathon Swimming Hall of Fame, which is based in Fort Lauderdale, United States, for their considerable prowess on water.

Joe and Norman are rightly proud of being "old school" swimmers. All their Channel and lake swims were conducted under the strict guidelines of the Channel Swimming Association (CSA) and British Long Distance Swimming Association (BLDSA) respectively. For all their differences, both Codes have one thing in common: the absolute abhorrence of wet suits.

Although they no longer Channel swim, their appetite for the sport is clearly undiminished and they still continue to mentor potential Channel swimmers and offer much sought after advice and encouragement. Although they are far too modest and unassuming to boast of their past glories, I feel that I must record something of their achievements.

Rochdale born Joe is obviously proud of being the oldest British citizen to swim the English Channel. He achieved this at the age of 65 in September

1999 in a time of 14 hours 9 minutes. In the 1950s and 1960s he was a stalwart of the BLDSA, winning most of their major championships, including the annual Windermere "end to end". He previously made two unsuccessful attempts on the Channel in 1961 and 1962. Despite being in his late 70s (when we meet) he admits to still swimming daily in the sea off Deal, where he now lives, "for fun".

Local born Norman is the epitome of what you'd think a Channel swimmer should look like. Solidly built and barrel chested to boot, he has the pedigree to prove it, having successfully completed three solo crossings of the Channel in 1967, 1971 & 1972. He is also a celebrated veteran of Windermere.

They are evidently keen to show me their labours and Joe has kindly selected some photographs of past Manchester swimmers attempting the Channel to whet my appetite and start the ball rolling.

Clearly theirs is a labour of love, as they are both dedicated to systematically cataloguing and cross referencing countless faded press cuttings, untitled sepia photographs, leather bound records and numerous anecdotes. It is painstaking work but they are determined to record for posterity and display as much as possible "on-line".

It is breath taking to hear of their experiences and I admit to eagerly grasping any titbits offered, no matter how casually or flippantly they are thrown about in general conversation. Consider the point made about landing on the French side, be it the difficulties of landing boats at Cap Gris Nez, the nearest point to England; missing Sangatte because of the strong currents or the issues of jelly fish in the Bay of Wissant. And as for the marine life? Joe even mentioned encountering a bemused grey seal mid Channel!

Norman is particularly emphatic about the criteria for success. "It's a mind-set," he implores, before adding how, "You swim 90% of the Channel with your head and 10% with your body". You sense his despair with some of those "top class" swimmers who just couldn't handle the enormity of the task-in-hand and packed up within 30 minutes of starting, not to mention the considerable investment in accompanying pilot boat, Channel Swimming Association and preparation.

However he is very proud of nurturing his many successes and tells me of some of the subtle tactics he employed to encourage some faltering swimmers to press ahead in the first vital half hour of the swim.

Although the Channel may be only 20 nautical miles wide at its narrowest point between Shakespeare Beach, near Dover, and Cap Gris Nez in France, such are the contradictory tides that swimmers must be prepared to undertake a circuitous route that can be anything between 30 and 35 miles long.

And of course the swimmer also needed to be prepared for the cold sea water! Norman couldn't stress enough the importance of being sufficiently acclimatised to the temperatures involved, although he admitted not liking to swim in waters below 53 or 54 degrees Fahrenheit.

And that's cold, by anyone's standards. But the final word on this subject must rest with Joe who had previously told me of past winter training endeavours in Hollingworth Lake, when he still lived in Rochdale, Lancashire.

I positively shivered as he told me that he sometimes had to break the ice in the middle of winter before he could even start to swim.

"But that wasn't the worst of it!" he quipped.

"Why, what was that", I responded naively as he prepared to deliver his punch line.

"Scallywags throwing snow balls at me!" he growled, indignantly.

It's time to shake hands and bid a very grateful farewell. I cannot thank Joe and Norman enough for giving up their time and sharing some of their memories and experiences. As well as inspiring me with their endeavours they have taught me an invaluable lesson which I will do well to remember for my future swims; the criteria for success in long distance swimming are as much to do with one's mind-set as one's physical ability.

SAFETY IS PARAMOUNT

Of course open water swimming on its day can be a wonderful and life changing experience, but it comes with considerable risks. I just can't stress how different open water swimming is from pool swimming.

I am reminded of a famous Olympic and World Championship medal winner who shall remain nameless but once admitted to me that he had tried open water swimming but found it far too cold for his liking. So if he struggles in open water then heaven help all those novice swimmers who decide to take up the challenge!

And please, don't get me started on the whys and wherefores of TV celebrity Davina McCall swimming across the near freezing width of Windermere in an attempt to raise money for the 2014 Sport Relief Triathlon. Good cause it certainly is but what she was putting herself through looked absolutely horrendous....

It is vitally important that certain specific rules and guidelines are applied, not matter how accomplished, self-confident or experienced a swimmer you consider yourself.

It's a sobering fact of life that temperatures are so much lower than in the heated municipal pool and that can lead to some open water novices being seriously troubled with breathing difficulties and cramping of muscles in the arms and legs. It can even lead to hypothermia.

Open water, after all, is an alien and uncompromising medium; you are on your own and you need to be able to cope with all eventualities. Attitude is all important; you need to be patient, flexible and prepared to change your plans should conditions deteriorate or unexpected challenges arise.

Of course it is useful to have a good swimming technique, but it is also fundamental that you bother to put in the hours pre swim in various pools, rivers and lakes to accustom yourself to the temperatures.

It is unfortunate that many accomplished pool swimmers are put off open water swimming for all the wrong reasons. Others seem too easily distracted by any number of sensible concerns and irrational fears. Their concerns are well documented: the size and depth of the lake playing on their mind; the off putting coldness and lack of clarity of the water; and, the disturbing effect of waves and wind on progress. Equally, anxieties over donning a "too tight" wet suit for the very first time, allied with real concerns over its ability to restrict breathing, never mind movement, all take their toll.

It's perfectly understandable. There is an awful lot to take in and master very quickly. And not everyone is confident enough to give up control and respond to prevailing conditions. However, all these perfectly sensible concerns can be mastered given time by good example, practice and encouragement.

But as for those irrational fears regarding "what may be lurking down below"! These fears are often shared with an accompanying groan and impassioned shiver of the shoulders for good effect. Well, let's just hope that these fears can be overcome by the swimmers' growing self-confidence and their realisation that the film "Jaws" could never have been made in Great Britain!

Unfortunately, very little can be done about those desperately long and perfectly harmless strands of algae which lurk in some of the lakes and make a habit of wrapping around swimmers' arms and legs with dreadful effect!

It is imperative that swimmers prepare adequately, including an appropriate Risk Assessment and prepare a sensible and practical contingency plan in case things don't go according to plan. I can't stress enough the need to inform and liaise with the following organisations at the very least well before starting any lake swim which affects the following:

- Lake District National Park Authority (LDNPA) Lake Ranger Team- for Windermere, Ullswater, Coniston Water and Derwent Water: (0844-2252922/01539-724555)

- South Lakeland District Council (SLDC) Lake Warden (for Windermere: 015394-42753)

- Ferry Companies

- Sailing Clubs

It is also important to abide by the rules and bye laws and restrictions of private landowners, the LDNPA, United Utilities and National Trust, etc. in my swims. Unfortunately, some swimmers give the sport a bad name and I include a couple of examples to give you a flavour of what I mean.

- An impromptu mass swim across Ullswater disrupting a prestigious Junior European yacht regatta organised by Ullswater Sailing Club. If only the organisers of the swim had bothered to inform other lake users of their plans and cared to check the suitability of the date and time of their swim.

- The organisers of a well-advertised and planned mass swim in Derwent Water "forgetting" to inform or consult the Keswick Launch Company with their race plans! And that was despite the organisers handing a 27 page (yes, twenty seven page!) Risk Assessment to all and sundry!

I have also attempted to include some "DOs and DON'Ts" which hopefully will help you enjoy swimming safely in open water on the next page. This is not an exhaustive list but serves as a timely reminder of what you may need. And, of course, there are all number of really useful web sites and Apps which will provide information relating to water quality, weather and whatever.

Of course if you have the slightest doubt or concern about your physical condition then you should always seek medical advice even before thinking about taking up any form of swimming.

DOS AND DON'TS

Open water swimmers should:

- Wear a wet suit

- Wear a brightly coloured cap and tow a bright safety tow float

- Be accompanied by a canoe or small boat with a white and blue alpha flag

- Never swim after consuming food and/or alcohol. That IS asking for trouble!

- Check water quality

- Prepare a Risk Assessment

- Plan where you are going to enter and leave the water.

- Read the signs; if they say swimming is not permitted then swimming is definitely not permitted!

- Tell someone where you are going and when you expect to be back

- Always enter the water slowly, to check the depth of water, irregularity of the bed and help the body adjust to chilly temperatures

- Never jump in

- Never swim alone

- Look out for other lake users; they may not be expecting to see a swimmer!

- Avoid mooring areas, marinas and jetties used by boats, ferry routes and boating channels

- Only swim when weather conditions are suitable-remember that conditions can rapidly change

- Check that your mobile phone has coverage. If it doesn't, do you know where the nearest land line is, in case of emergency?

- Remember to check, clean and dry all your swim kit to avoid contamination

- Last and most important...enjoy yourself!

YEAR ONE
ON YOUR MARKS....

Is it any wonder that I'm slightly apprehensive about what I have taken on?
Even though I have previously taken part in any number of 5 kilometre
sponsored pool swims on behalf of Duncan Goodhew's "Swimathon"
charity I realise that the prospect of taking on Coniston Water, which is a
numbing five and a quarter miles long, is starting to concern me. And the
least said about tackling Ullswater's seven and a quarter miles, never mind
Windermere's formidable ten and a half miles length, the better!

Nevertheless, I take heart from Joe and Norman's advice and I decide to
begin with some of the lesser lakes in an attempt to build up my stamina
and strength. Above all I want to enjoy the journey. As I'm not intending
to break any records with my challenge I decide to divide the lakes into
what I believe is a manageable group of swims per year, bearing in mind
vagaries of the notorious Cumbrian weather, arranging boat crews and
whatever. Accordingly I split the 17 lakes into three groups and plan to do
a similar number of lakes in each of three consecutive years.

I try and "recce" each lake before taking part in a swim This usually involves checking out the lake shore access, as well as clarifying the location of toilets, parking facilities and public telephones. All this information could prove essential in the event of an emergency occurring.

I find the four Ordnance Survey 1:25 000 scale Explorer Maps, reference OL4, 5, 6 & 7, covering the Lake District, very useful for identifying the best locations for entering and exiting the lake, as well as locating safety refuges where swimmers can land if the need arises. I would also recommend that swimmers acquire a set of the large scale lake plans produced by the Lake District National Park Authority as they mark those lengths of the shore which are open to the public and those which are private. These are generally available in the Tourist Information Centres.

This "recce" can also help monitor prevailing conditions and ensure that selected routes are achievable. I quote, from experience, the time that my group of swimming friends considered swimming the lengths of Grasmere and the adjoining Rydal Water "in one go". The scheme may have sounded highly desirable "on paper", but my pre-swim recce proved just how difficult this task would prove to be at that particular time of the year on account of very low water levels and the presence of aggressive swans. Although it might just have been feasible to "slither, slide and stumble" the length of the near dry and boulder strewn river bed linking the lakes, there was no way that I was going to run the gauntlet of the pair of nesting swans guarding the entrance to Rydal Water!

I must stress that swimmers should not assume that the locations noted and access routes identified in the book, and on the accompanying illustrations, are on public land or denote rights of way. If in doubt, swimmers must check and seek permission.

INTRODUCTORY COURSE TO OPEN WATER SWIMMING

Saturday 31 May 2014

Keen to ensure that I start my Lake District Challenge with good intent, I sign up for a half day "Introductory Course to Open Swimming" with Ambleside based leisure company, "Swim the Lakes" at the end of May. (2 Compston Road, Ambleside, Cumbria. 015394 33826).

It proves to be an ideal refresher and tonic for my future plans. Indeed, I would recommend any novice swimmer considering lake swimming for the very first time or, for that matter, any experienced swimmer wishing to brush up their skills to consider booking on this or a similar course.

Co-presenters, Pete and Andrea, are both accomplished swimmers and prove to be excellent guides. They tailor
their extensive course material to
suit the varied needs, abilities
and considerable age
range of our 15 strong
group. They exhibit a
remarkable sensitivity
and understanding of all
our separate needs, be they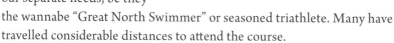
the wannabe "Great North Swimmer" or seasoned triathlete. Many have travelled considerable distances to attend the course.

Andrea begins with theory and instils the need for all open swimmers to take responsibility for their actions and ensure that they are both confident and aware of the environment. There is so much to take in. And I must admit that Pete's demonstration on the correct way to put on a wet suit proves to be a salutary lesson in everything that I have been doing wrong for so many years!

Afterwards, we head over to nearby Rydal Water to put theory into practice. Even though it's a quiet lake at the best of times, safety canoes guard our initial entries into the water. There is plenty of time to acclimatise to the cold water and relax before we are put through our paces.

Different exercises are progressed to suits the needs of the swimmers. Steadily, we focus and develop skills necessary for open water swimming; there is a very real need to improve our breathing, lengthen our strokes and improve our (hopeless) directional skills!

After an enjoyable segment of rehearsing racing starts, we conclude the "practical" with a celebratory circuit of Heron Island. Naturally, some of the freestylers rapidly disappear in a frenzy of whirring arms and brightly coloured swimming caps with "Swim The Lakes" motifs. Is it any wonder that the resident duck population takes urgent flight, in response?

It's time to get out and retire to the conveniently located "Badger Bar" for a chat and well-earned cup of coffee.

NB Boats aren't normally allowed on Rydal Water and swimmers are asked to avoid the northern shores.

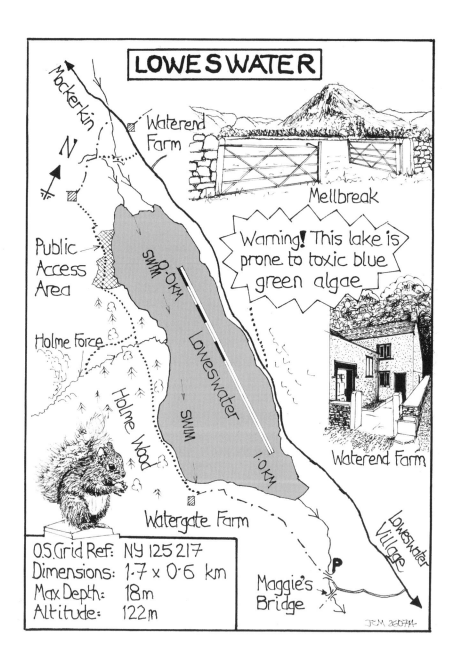

LOWESWATER

Mockerkin

N

Waterend Farm

Mellbreak

Warning! This lake is prone to toxic blue green algae

Public Access Area

0·0KM

SWIM

Loweswater

SWIM

1·0KM

Holme Force

Holme Wood

Waterend Farm

Watergate Farm

Loweswater Village

O.S. Grid Ref: NY 125 217
Dimensions: 1·7 x 0·6 km
Max Depth: 18m
Altitude: 122m

Maggie's Bridge

P

JCM 26.07.11

LOWESWATER (1/17)

Tuesday 3 June 2014

What a glorious evening to be swimming the length of Loweswater! Situated in the remote west of the Lake District, this charming mile long water shelters in a near hidden, working valley largely bypassed by mass tourism. Even the challenges of climbing Darling Fell and Carling Knott seem to barely register with most fell walkers.

I want the first swim to be a little special; to inaugurate my Lake District Swim Challenge, and I am delighted that this swim proves to be the ideal inspiration for the considerable challenges that lie ahead!

Tom, Paul and James join me for the swim. We meet at Maggie's Bridge Car Park, at the southern end of the lake (OS Grid Ref: NY135210) and change in the lee of Watergate Farm, besides a long line of abandoned timber rowing boats; clinker clad to boot! How sad that they no longer "ply their trade" over the lake; I once enjoyed a superb autumn's day rowing one of these boats with the lake all to myself. The lake is owned by the National Trust.

Colleagues arrive in dribs and drabs to support the unfolding spectacle, lend assistance and, unfortunately, laugh at my desperate attempts at donning my wet suit…. It's not the easiest of places to find and we seem to have lost Ricky en route. Try as we might, but it proves impossible to raise a mobile signal.

But where to swim? Much of the lake shore is difficult to access and we follow the delightful wooded southern shore line path through Holme Wood to the far bay designated "Access to Lake Shore" (OS Grid Ref:NY118221). Dare anyone not be enchanted by Holme Wood! It's famous in these parts for its luscious carpet of wild flowers in the spring and haunt of endangered red squirrels.

And so to water. The bay proves very shallow and we paddle a long way out to gain the western extreme of the lake to say that "we've done the whole lake"; well, as far as we can without grounding on a silty bed and stirring any more of that muddy sediment than is absolutely necessary.

Pity, then, that the water should prove so dark, peaty and surprisingly chilly "12 degrees!" announces James. And he should know, as he's had his fair share of successful exploits. As well as coming third in his first attempt at tackling the Keswick triathlon, his tales of mountain biking in Austria and "hard core" swimming in the winter are legendary.

Admittedly, the water feels a shade nippier than last Saturday's practice dip in Rydal Water. Fortunately, there does not appear to be any of the blessed blue green algae-bloom in sight, although I am reliably informed that it can occur on this lake at any time. Visitors beware: whilst it might be harmful to humans, it can be lethal to animals.

Bright swimming caps are fitted and goggles finally adjusted as we push off. Even though it is not intended to be a race James powers ahead, closely followed by a surprisingly nippy Tom. And I always thought that he was more at home caving in the deepest of caverns rather than exercising on open water; now he has impressed me!

Our plan is well rehearsed, to follow the southern shoreline and head for the wooded headland jutting out into the centre of the lake, before heading directly for Watergate Farm at the far end of the lake.

It takes a few minutes for my feet to warm up but quickly I get into my stride. It is truly wonderful afloat; it is difficult to convey the sheer delight of being alone mid water. And such views! The surrounding fells appear mirrored in the stillness of flat, calm waters.

And as for the silence; that all embracing dry stone wall to wall silence that literally takes your breath away. Noises are amplified eerily, be they the explosive clatter of distant tractor racing over roadside cattle grid or the methodical beat of solitary cormorant as it races with outstretched neck barely skimming the water's surface.

Paul is a natural athlete, proficient in rugby, cycling and fell running. He swims just ahead and occasionally stops to check that I am alright, which is greatly appreciated and, I suppose expected, considering that I am at least 25 years older than my friends....

Colleagues follow closely along the shoreline, to record our progress and return our footwear. On reaching the wooded headland, mid lake, I change direction and now steer directly for the unassuming bulk of Mellbreak straight ahead.

We press on regardless with a steady, easy pace beside an endless wooded shoreline. Even though the final quarter mile seems to last for ever, I tell myself to be wary; distances on the water can be deceptive and I have long learned the folly of pushing on too far out.

Impetuously, I power into a full blooded racing stroke for the final, vital few strokes. Colleagues and the other three swimmers lining the shore greet my arrival with well-meaning applause as I ground solidly onto the rising lake bed. Success! I have finally run out of water (OS Grid Ref: NY126212).

This has been a cracking swim and we seem to make sure that there is plenty of time for photographs and poses before the arduous tasks of removing and slushing out wet suits. Try as I might, I always seem to need a hand to assist....

The evening continues. Dave B, who evidently knows quite a lot about these things, recommends that we head over to the nearby Kirkstile Inn for a celebratory pint of "Loweswater Gold" real ale and meal of steak pie with all the trimmings. What a good idea! And I am delighted that in the course of the evening my colleagues are asking where we are swimming next!

NB The West Cumbria Rivers Trust later report in 2016 that salmon have returned to Loweswater for the first time in years! They believe that this is a good sign that their Loweswater Care Programme appears to be working; this was undertaken to reduce the amount of harmful phosphorus entering the lake and its tributaries, thus improving the quality of water and reducing the amount of algae present.

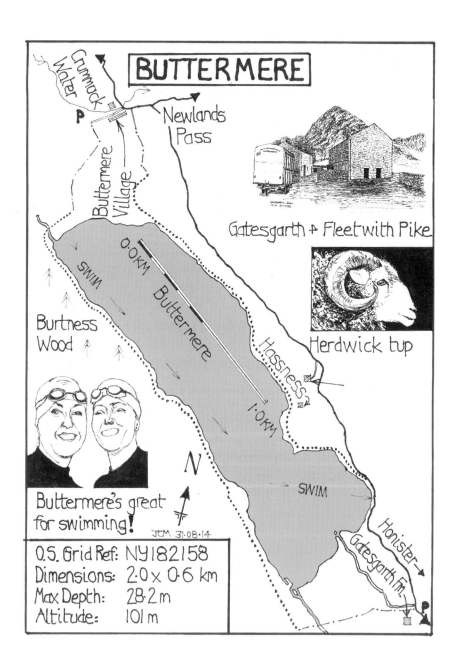

BUTTERMERE

Crummock Water

P

Newlands Pass

Buttermere Village

0.0 KM Buttermere

SWIM

Burtness Wood

Hassness?

1.0 KM

Gatesgarth & Fleetwith Pike

Herdwick tup

N

SWIM

Honister →

Gatesgarth Fm.

P

Buttermere's great for swimming!

JCM 31·08·14

O.S. Grid Ref: NY182158
Dimensions: 2.0 × 0.6 km
Max Depth: 28.2 m
Altitude: 101 m

BUTTERMERE (2/17)

Tuesday 17 June 2014

It seems fitting that we should now turn our attention to Buttermere, a near neighbour of Loweswater. Buttermere, a little over a mile long, is situated in one of the most beautiful and dramatic valleys in the whole of the Lake District. So it's no real wonder that it's assumed something of the role of mecca for wild water swimmers. Rarely a weekend seems to pass by in the summer without its crystal clear waters hosting one organised charity event or another.

We are blessed with another lovely night for our swim! It is encouraging to find that we have gained another swimmer, Adam, as well as a couple of paddlers, Mike and Paul B, to accompany us and offer much welcome encouragement.

I take the opportunity to drive over to Buttermere well in advance of my colleagues' intended arrival, to obtain a couple of obligatory National Trust permits for our supporting canoes (£5 per canoe) from the car park machine located in the National Trust car park in Buttermere.

And there's plenty of time for a pot of tea in Croft Farm café, located in the centre of the village, as well. "You're swimming in the lake?" the owner queries before adding with a chuckle, "Well this will keep you going!" as she hands me a plain buttered scone fresh out of the oven. And it does, believe you me!

No-one appears to bat an eyelid as we change into wet suits in the village centre and make our way down the farm lane to the pebble lined lake shore. Our plan is clear and precise: to swim the length of the lake from the north western shingle bay (OS Grid Ref: NY173163) to the south eastern roadside (OS Grid Ref: NY191154), alongside the delightfully wood lined southern shore. "Against the current?" teases James.

Some remark that the lake's setting, sunk deep in a cleft of mountains, reminds them of a Norwegian fjord. So it's not really that surprising to learn that many of the local farming community can boast of having descended from Vikings who settled here in large numbers in the 9th and 10th centuries.

Buttermere's appeal to the outside world is nothing new. The village even attracted some of the first tourists to the Lake District at the start of the 19th century. And they had to be intrepid to brave the mountain passes which then led from Keswick! Most were drawn to see Mary Robinson, the celebrated "Maid of Buttermere", daughter of mine landlord of "The Fish". Although lauded by the Lake Poets, she endured the cruel tragedy of marriage to a forger and self-seeking bigamist.

And, once the boats join us, we can begin! Mike knows the lakes like the proverbial back of his hand and recommends that we follow the "western channel" where the water is deepest! As well as a stalwart of Carlisle Canoe Club, he is a qualified life guard and has spent a considerable number of weekends supervising swimmers on "Great North Swims" and whatever in the Lakes. But the less said about those harrowing stories of some swimmers' lack of preparation and foolhardiness, the better!

We are really pleased that Adam's joined us and keen to give it a go. Even though we tease him for his curious attire, consisting of a wetsuit vest and florid Bermuda shorts that might appear more at home in Ibiza than Cumbria, we're desperately keen to support him. We purposefully take our time to get into our stride; although the water is surprisingly warm for so early in the season, I struggle for the first quarter mile. But once Mike joins me in his paddle, I seriously get into my stride and my stroke lengthens.

We have the lake very much to ourselves. What a wonderful night to be swimming in such flat, calm water! And it is sublime, just sublime. Water flows imperceptibly, inaudibly and at ease. There is something gloriously elemental and reassuring with being on water and surrounded by such storm tossed peaks.

This valley never ceases to delight. Over the years, I must have walked on most of the peaks on view and swum in many of the surrounding upland tarns but one of my most memorable trips involved spending a glorious lazy, hazy summer's day "messing about" on the lake in one of the National Trust's row boats. It  felt wonderful to leave the boat's keel to its own devices whilst swallows darted dementedly all around and fish rose for air. Dare I imagine them to be arctic char coming up for vital air, that ancient fish known to inhabit the depths of lake?

We all settle into our pace. Whilst James and Tom have long vanished over the southern horizon, Paul remains close in front. I'm pleased to hear that Adam is still hanging on and being shadowed closely by Paul B, an accomplished wind surfer and fine rock guitarist, in his canoe.

And so this wonderful swim continues. By the time I pass Dalegarth, set within the northern wooded shores, I realise that I have made half way; it's a clarion call to power up my stroke and begin the long push "for home", aiming for the prickly spine of Fleetwith Pike, rising proudly to the south of the lake.

"Aim for that building below the cleft in the hills" Mike demands as I adjust my line as I make my final approach to the southern shore where I meet the other three swimmers who have already landed.

Rather than taking off our wetsuits, we all head back into the lake to escort and encourage Adam the last desperate 100 metres of the lake. We are delighted that he manages to complete the lake swim in less than sixty minutes.

GRASMERE (3/17)

Tuesday 01 July 2014

"…the loveliest spot that man hath ever found…" William Wordsworth (1770–1850)

Tom, James and Adam join me for a swim in Grasmere early one summer evening after work. After all it would seem criminal not to make the most of such a heaven sent evening, with the clearest blue sky and non-existent wind. It's a time when the lakes are their most enjoyable and roads their quietest.

But isn't it funny how appearances can be so deceptive? Even though I have enjoyed some glorious carefree days rowing on Grasmere's apparently tranquil waters in the past, I could never have anticipated that our swim would prove to be so taxing or present so many unexpected challenges!

Of course the village of Grasmere is a little special. Thank goodness it still manages to retain a refreshing originality with more than its fair share of art galleries, bookshops and upmarket tea shops. Of course it will forever be associated with William Wordsworth, England's greatest lyric poet. William spent a total of 14 years living in Grasmere. But it is the time spent in Dove Cottage that is most popularly associated with him and has now become a place of some considerable literary pilgrimage.

Wordsworth dedicated his eight years living in this little cottage, "crammed edge full" with people, to "…plain living but high poetry…". It seemed to work, because he wrote some of the greatest poetry in the English language here. Goodness knows though what the nosey neighbours must have thought of him sharing this cramped cottage with both Dorothy, his obsessively devoted sister, and his wife, Mary, nee Hutchinson.

But back to the job in hand. We park in the road at Red Bank and chase the plunging forest track down to lake shore. A generous length of shingle strewn beach lining the south eastern corner of the lake beside the River

25

Rydal outlet makes an ideal location for the start of our swim (OS Grid Ref NY342058).

Although this beach can be very busy at weekends and in the holidays, it is near deserted as we change into our kit. Even though I have completed several successful tarn dips in my newish three quarter length "shortie" wet suit, I still manage to stick my left leg down the right arm socket at the first attempt at fitting....

The lake is comparatively small, being less than a mile long and roughly triangular in shape. We decide to "pair up" as we haven't any boat support. Whilst Tom and James intend to do a full clockwise circuit of the lake, Adam and I decide to swim the western side, which is approximately 0.75miles long.

We are in good company. After all, the Wordsworths kept a boat on Grasmere and were famous in these parts for "...drifting, reciting or reading aloud". Dorothy once chronicled that "...after tea we rowed down to Loughrigg Fell, visited the white fox gloves, gathered wild strawberries and walked up to view Ryedale".

And lovely it sounds too. Certainly views on the night are wonderful; be they of those glorious woodlands and gentle hills surrounding, complete with Victorian piles loitering shyly behind dense rhododendron, or of the distant, spectacular forms of Helm Crag and Nab Scar.

Nevertheless, problems arise as soon as we "dip our toes" and find that the shore line abruptly plummets over a lip of broken boulders into deep water! This nasty little drop could well prove perilous to non-swimmers. And there are even more submerged hazards to watch out for. "Avoid the tree stump!" Tom cries out. Ouch, too late! No matter, James is already powering away...

The surface is delightful! Scarcely a ripple, never mind a rogue wave, disturbs the flat, calmest of benign water surfaces imaginable. Adam is setting a cracking pace with an effortless freestyle and I struggle to keep up. Soon we settle into a steady routine, although we find that we are running a gauntlet of dense tangling weeds as we approach the densely wooded island. It is an opportunity to halt, catch breath and struggle out of their grip!

The lake of Grasmere may appear to be an enchanted water, deep blue watered and ringed by lush verdant growth, but I have to ask how healthy can the murky water be? The water quality can't be helped by the presence of all those Canada geese lining the north western shore. Their numbers were culled several years ago because it was argued that their poo was poisoning the lake and killing off the resident fish.

Light from the fading sun dazzles as we approach the remote, reed littered north western shore. It is an opportunity to rest and talk with a couple of women taking an impromptu dip and break from their punishing schedule on the Coast to Coast walk.

We decide to return by rounding the far, eastern side of the island, little realising how difficult or taxing this would prove to be. Perhaps we should have realised that the presence of all those dead trees floating in the water was a sign of something amiss. Nevertheless, we had never bargained for the bed to be so shallow or silt laden; it was un-swimmable, in other words.

I have to ask: could this be the same "lovely" island that so captivated Samuel Taylor Coleridge on a visit to attend an evening's bonfire and "idyllic picnic" with the Wordsworths so many years ago. I fear so.....

We are forced to return. Is it any wonder that Adam has now had more than enough and decides to head back to the shore and walk back? It is a sensible decision. The night is still young and I decide to swim back to the start point. Progress is near effortless and it proves a wonderful experience, with sun's fading grandeur generously illuminating the tree lined island.

Nevertheless, I listen aghast as Tom and James recount their desperate journey around the far side of the island; they were reduced more than once to lying on their fronts and literally clawing their way over dense silt and impenetrable weeds. What would William Wordsworth have made of that, I must say?

HOW CLEAN ARE CUMBRIA'S LAKES?

I experience so many variations in the cleanliness of lake water that I wonder if there can really be a problem with the water quality of some of our Cumbrian lakes.

Of course it concerns me. Although I am not qualified to comment on the extent or seriousness of the issues of water quality there is no doubt that the beauty and, intrinsically, the health of all the Lakes are fundamental to the well-being of Cumbria and the sustainability of the tourist industry.

Grasmere would not appear alone. The Lake District National Park Authority has admitted that Windermere's water quality has been declining for many years. So concerned are they by the effect it is having on several native plants and animals, whilst encouraging some non-native plants in the bargain, that it recently initiated the grandly titled "Windermere Catchment Restoration Programme" to improve matters.

The seriousness of the situation really hit home in 2010 when the organisers of the Great North Swim had to cancel that year's event in Windermere due to the build-up of high phosphate levels. They believed that the presence of toxic blue-green algae in the lake could have been dangerous to the 9,000 competitors intending to take part in the event.

The Lake District National Park Authority has established, over the last few years, any number of wide ranging initiatives and partnerships with national bodies, companies and landowners involved in the Lake District to develop ways of improving water quality. Fortunately, most schemes now appear to be bearing fruit and significantly reducing the amount of phosphates entering many of the lakes; it augurs well for the future.

There is no room for complacency. The Authority was so concerned by a drastic deterioration of the quality of Bassenthwaite Lake's water in recent years that they were once forced to declare that the lake was "in the balance" and initiated the "Still Waters, Bassenthwaite Lake Restoration Programme" to improve matters.

And there are other issues, not least the spread of invasive non-native species (INNS). An alien plant called Australian swamp crop, or New Zealand 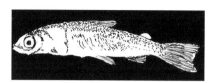 pigmyweed, is proving a particular threat to Lake District wildlife. Growth is phenomenal and I can vouch that it is already invading and causing damage in the so called "nutrient rich" waters of many of our lakes.

I take the opportunity to cite the aims of the West Cumbria Rivers Trust, which urges all swimmers to take time and care to check, clean and dry their swimming kit thoroughly before and after swimming. The Trust strives, tirelessly, to restore and enhance the value of rivers, lakes, estuaries and surrounding countryside throughout West Cumbria for the benefit of people and wildlife.

It also recommends that swimmers should remove any plant matter or aquatic life that may have attached themselves. It is vital that such invasive plants and aquatic life are not allowed to spread or cross into unaffected lakes or waterways.

The phenomenal growth in open water swimming presents particular problems. One weekend a swimmer can be in the West Country, the next in Scotland; so imagine the potential for the transference of invasive plants across country....

CRUMMOCK WATER

Scale Hill

Lanthwaite Wood

Cockermouth

SWIM

0.0

Crummock Water

1.0 KM

Looking South

N

Heron

SWIM

Hause Point

Buttermere

Cumberland + Westmorland wrestling

Scale Force Waterfall

O.S. Grid Ref: NY 158 190
Dimensions: 4·2 × 0·9 km
Max Depth: 43 m
Altitude: 99 m

JCM 24·11·14

CRUMMOCK WATER (4/17)

Tuesday 8 July 2014

Having tested ourselves with introductory swims of Loweswater, Buttermere and Grasmere, it only seems appropriate that we should now turn our attention to Crummock Water, the largest of the three lakes occupying the Vale of Lorton. Make no mistake: this is an ambitious undertaking as Crummock Water measures 2.5 miles from end to end, as the dolphin swims.

All lakes present their own unique challenges and issues. Nevertheless, planning this swim proves particularly irksome. Perhaps I'm conscious of the distances involved and also concerned by a definite change in the weather?

After all Crummock Water is regarded as "a cold lake" by those who know about these things. And water temperatures are not helped by last weekend's torrential downpours. Whilst sudden change may provide welcome substance to pointless pleasantries between good natured neighbours, they can have serious impact on the fortunes of the unprepared open water swimmer.

Fortunately, Tom, Adam and I seem to be blessed with a calm, balmy evening as we park at the National Trust Car Park in the woods opposite Scalehill Bridge (OS Grid Ref: NY149215) and begin to change into trunks and wetsuits.

Though, heaven knows what that earnest couple of binocular clad ornithologists, returning to their parked car at the wrong time, make of Adam sauntering the car park resplendent in a bright blue wet suit bought in "Sainsbury's" for a princely £30 the other Saturday night. Oh, yes, Adam at his sartorial best is definite competition for our debonair James in his "Blue 70" wetsuit. Now, come to think about it: where is James? Ah, at last he arrives, breathless from delays at work. We three pile into his car and head for Woodhouse, near the southern base of the lake.

I was going to say that this 5 mile trip went without incident but I can't. And any good natured "ribbing" quickly evaporates as we finally chance upon the lake as we drive the road hugging Crummock Water's eastern shore and note its wind whipped waters. Oh, goodness, this is not what we expected, at all…..

We are fortunate that a canoeing friend, Andy, has agreed to accompany us with his inflatable canoe, inappropriately named "Palava", tonight. It is reassuring to see that he is already parked-up and energetically inflating this dark green canoe with an outsized bicycle pump as we meet at the roadside near the southern end of the lake. We have previously purchased the obligatory National Trust "all day" canoe permit for £5.00 from the National Trust car park in Buttermere.

Our car park is an unusually busy spot for a mid-week evening. As well as Andy, I'm pleased to "meet and greet" Richard and Janet, husband and wife swimmers from Carlisle. Small world indeed! They are already "wet-suited" up and also preparing to venture into the lake on their own. Isn't it curious how our paths keep on crossing!

We follow the southern shoreline to the broad sweep of shingle beach besides the inlet of the River Cocker (OS Grid Ref: NY167175). How curious that the adjoining row of NT rowing boats beached above the high water mark should prompt such a flood of memories of the last time I rowed on the lake on a sweltering summer's afternoon!

What a time for James to realise that he's left his hat and goggles in the car; back he heads off to retrieve the offending items.

Sitting within a deep glacial trough, Crummock Water is curved and best likened to a boomerang with two unequal wings or stretches. We start our swim at the base of the shorter, southern section. It is an easy entrance into gradually deepening water. Although the water feels reasonably warm, we all too quickly encounter a frenzy of wind whipped waves. It proves surprisingly choppy and I gulp down more than enough water to last a life time in the first 100 metres as I struggle to co-ordinate my normally ever reliable racing breaststroke and attempt to snatch breaths of desperate air between rogue waves.

This is really scary! I admit that my decision to swim from south to north with the current is greatly influenced by those signs warning of "strong currents and deep water" in the northern bay. However, I had not taken into account the strength of the prevailing westerly wind. No matter, Tom and Adam start to power away, in seemingly effortless freestyle.

They do say that it is important to experience the Lake District in all its majestic moods and wretched conditions. But I have to say that the gruelling half mile swim to Hause Point takes the biscuit! With random waves smacking into my face and crashing all over my body, I really wonder if we'd made the right decision to swim tonight.

No matter, we'd started, so we might as well finish. And thankfully Andy arrives aboard his gleaming canoe in the nick of time. His presence is incredibly reassuring and I am pleased that he accompanies me northwards for the rest of the swim.

Somewhere James powers past, reunited with brightest yellow cap and goggles, racing freestyle like a man possessed.

Slowly, but steadily, we gain the shelter of Hause Point, that iconic cliff face rearing out of the eastern shore at the base of the dramatic Rannerdale Knotts, just below the point where the shore road ducks under an overhanging rock face.

Even though Crummock Water is renowned for its incredible water clarity – a result of low nutrient status, great depth and low temperatures – I still manage to collide with a subterranean rock boulder as I round close to the Point. Ouch!

Fortunately, the wind drops as we round the Point and enter the longer, northern section of the lake. At last, normal swimming conditions are gratefully restored! It is time to realign and head for the distant northern end of the lake. And doesn't it look a long way! Lined by high, towering summits, the lake appears imposing, rather than intimate.

Swimmers should note that there isn't shore access for the first kilometre north of Rannerdale, and only a resident colony of Canada geese for raucous company. No, I would not recommend it!

Conditions have so improved that I can now really get into my racing breaststroke and start powering away. Practice certainly helps me swim like an automaton almost to the beat of a demented metronome as my stroke continues relentlessly.

A wonderful evening prevails. So silent and serene our journey continues. There's no doubt that you gain a different perspective from the water, and we are rewarded for all  our considerable efforts by stupendous views of Mellbreak's craggy ridge, not to mention the spectacular Ling Crag looming fearsomely over a low rocky promontory of a tombolo spilling miraculously in to the water.

"No need to hurry," chides Andy, as we catch up a tiring Adam. It's a great feeling to realise that with only a mile or so to go we should be able to complete the swim, barring disasters.

Cumbria suits Andy down to the ground; he's an accomplished mountaineer, skier, sailor and, of course, canoeist amongst many other things. I have known him for over twenty five years ever since he first moved "north" from Warwickshire.

We press on regardless, with Adam matching me stroke for stroke with his languid and near effortless crawl. Finally, I glimpse the wooded northern end of the lake, distant and hazy under a low setting sun. I try as I might to recall reference points to aim for and judge progress, but the near eastern wooded shoreline appears as featureless as unenticing....

"You're swimming far too close to the shoreline!" warns Andy. Twinges of cramp occasionally stab each calf; they are a warning that I'm pushing myself too hard. Andy's offer of a piece of banana goes down well with a large and unintentional mouthful of lake water.

The water chills noticeably and flows faster as we enter the final, narrow "stretch" of the lake. Passing the iconic masonry boat house, nestling beside a secret shingle beach within the wooded shoreline, spurs me to quicken my pace despite the finishing line being much further away than I can possibly imagine.

What a relief to realise that the final beach is looming dead ahead; James and Tom are standing at water's edge and welcoming both mine and Adam's successful arrival. Suddenly, I find myself gliding uncontrollably into a shallow pebble strewn beach. We've finally arrived (OS Grid Ref: NY152208). I try to stand up, but immediately fall over, as my balance is temporarily thrown by a combination of over exertion and wave action.

It is now approaching 9:00pm and the light is starting to fade. It's time for Andy to pack away the canoe and accompany us on the long walk back to the car parked at the far side of Lanthwaite Wood. After changing we drive back to Woodhouse to return Andy and canoe to his car and pick up our other car.

It has been another brilliant evening on the water.

RYDAL WATER

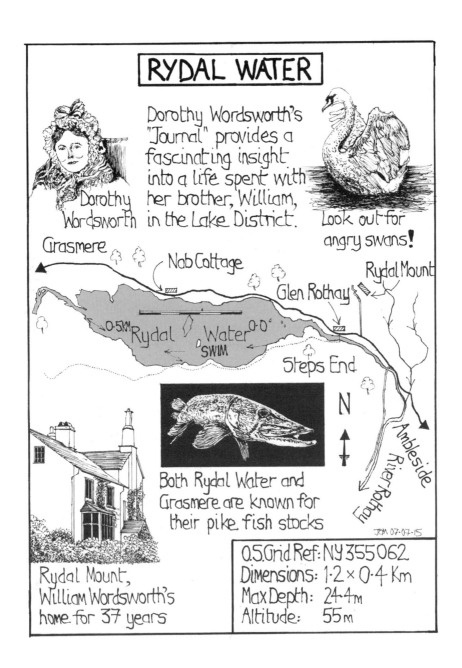

Dorothy Wordsworth's "Journal" provides a fascinating insight into a life spent with her brother, William, in the Lake District.

Dorothy Wordsworth

Look out for angry swans!

Grasmere

Nab Cottage

Rydal Mount

Glen Rothay

0.5km Rydal Water 0.0

SWIM

Steps End

N

Both Rydal Water and Grasmere are known for their pike fish stocks

Ambleside River Rothay

JCM 07·07·15

Rydal Mount, William Wordsworth's home for 37 years

O.S. Grid Ref: NY 355 062
Dimensions: 1·2 × 0·4 Km
Max Depth: 24·4 m
Altitude: 55 m

RYDAL WATER (5/17)

Sunday 27 July 2014

I am really pleased that my niece, Laura, wants to go open water swimming in the Lakes. Though heaven knows what she'll make of the experience, giving that she's just spent a week sun worshipping and swimming in Spain's crystal clear waters.

Admittedly, there is no better time to be swimming in Cumbria. The lakes are really starting to warm up and Coniston Water was reported to be a practically unheard of 20 degrees Centigrade, the other day!

I suggest we try Rydal Water for starters. Short of a mile long, Rydal Water is a most beguiling and largely ignored stretch of water. Even though the busy A591 skirts its northern shore, the motorist is tempted with only the briefest of views. This is a pity, because it really is a little gem.

Although there has been heavy rain overnight, bright sunshine greets our arrival. We follow the wooded path around the southern lake shore and head for a tiny, sheltered shingle beach situated the other side of a metal gate set in the dry stone wall (OS Grid Ref: NY360061). And it's still wonderfully deserted, well before the "Madding Crowds" have even breakfasted…

It is great to know that the water is warm enough to dispense with wetsuits and that we can swim comfortably just in "cossies". We intend to swim along the southern shore; Laura's Mum and Dad have come to offer support; follow our progress along the shore-lined path; and carry our kit.

Talk about "all splash and dash"! No sooner has Laura waded out to waist deep waters then she is away like a proverbial rocket. "Muggins" can only watch her distant progress at lake edge whilst he is still fiddling with goggles and swim cap....

Despite my best precautions, I still manage to bash my right knee on an errant boulder as I kick away powerfully from the beach. Ouch! We soon join up beside the nearest sandy headland and head towards the first of two islands, appropriately named Little Isle.

I feel so much more relaxed and accomplished an open water swimmer since the last time "I dipped my toes" in Rydal Water care of "Swim the Lakes" a couple of months ago. It certainly proves the point about putting in the miles.

There is no doubt about the water purity, judging by the copious clumps of water lilies at lake edge, although clarity is at best described as "soupy". Nevertheless, the novice swimmer must beware of those beguiling strands of green algae that have the nasty habit of wrapping themselves around arms and legs most disconcertingly.

I've encountered worse, and recall once becoming nearly entrapped in a forest of underwater kelp when snorkelling at Maiden's Bay, Girvan, with diving friends way back in my 20s. However, I perfectly understand Laura's concerns as she decides to head directly back to shore and retrieve

her kit from her Mum and Dad. She has done well, swimming so far in open water for the first time.

Beyond Heron Isle, the larger of the two islands, the water deepens and I decide to press on and savour these uncharted waters. Suffice to say, it

is a sheer delight to "open up" my racing stroke -
combining a powerful leg kick with a long relaxing
glide - and power out to mid water. Surely this is
wild swimming at its very best!

Intending to swim the whole length of the lake,
I aim for the far, western Grasmere inlet. I am
somewhat perturbed to realise that I appear to
be heading straight to a swan's nest, all massive
jumbled pile of sticks and gleaming owner standing
guard. Wisely, I decide to turn back with some
haste; and hope that I haven't ruffled too many
feathers in the process!

Stories of indignant swans attacking canoeists who
have strayed too close to their nests and breaking paddlers' arms with a
single sweep of their powerful wings may be legendary but I am taking no
chances!

It's been a good swim and I return to meet the family who are waiting
for me at water's edge (OS Grid Ref: NY355060). After celebrating our
successful trip with a belated breakfast and coffee in Grasmere, the
heavens open. Literally. Well it is the Lake District.

NB Boats are not allowed on the lake without permission. And access for
swimmers is only permitted from the southern shore.

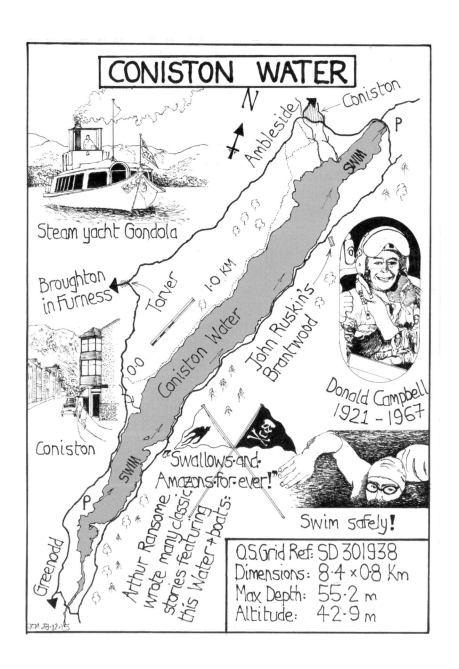

CONISTON WATER

N

Coniston

Ambleside

SWIM

P

Steam yacht Gondola

Broughton in Furness

Torver

1.0 KM

0.0

Coniston Water

John Ruskin's Brantwood

Donald Campbell
1921 – 1967

Coniston

"Swallows·and·
Amazons·for·ever!"

SWIM

P

Swim safely!

Greenodd

Arthur Ransome wrote many classic stories featuring this Water + boats.

O.S. Grid Ref:	SD 301938
Dimensions:	8·4 × 0·8 Km
Max Depth:	55·2 m
Altitude:	42·9 m

JCM 28·12·15

CONISTON WATER (6/17)

Saturday 06 September 2014

And now for the big one, Coniston Water end to end! My preparations are not helped by a current lack of "match practice". Regrettably, the wheels seem to have well and truly fallen off our Tuesday night swims as a result of work and family commitments.

A change in the weather hasn't exactly helped either. And so I decide to take part in an "Epic Events" organised 3.8 kilometre swim in the lake a month beforehand. Conditions are atrocious but the testing swim serves an ideal dress rehearsal for the "Chillswim" event. (There's more on "Epic Events" later in the book).

This is the second year that "Chillswim" have organised this end to end swim in Coniston Water. This mass participation swim is unique for being open to both wet suited and "bare-back" competitors and over four hundred swimmers have signed up, including a sprinkling of Channel Swimmers. Although I signed up for the lake swim early in the year, the reality of actually now swimming the entire 5.25mile length of Coniston Water in one go both excites and worries me.

I register for the swim at John Ruskin School in Coniston the night before the swim and am given an orange tow float together with my swim cap, wrist band, car stickers and various freebies.

Coniston is charming, a remote slate clad village dominated by the Old Man of Coniston at the north of the lake. Generations of families have been employed in the extensive slate quarrying industry and the village will forever be associated with John Ruskin's artistic aspirations and Donald Campbell's water speed records. It evokes all that is good and wholesome about the Lake District.

I camp overnight at the National Trust's Hoathwaite Farm site, overlooking the western lake shore and awake to glorious conditions for the swim. I rise early and drive over to the John Ruskin School to change

41

into my wet suit. I must also remember to clip the obligatory bright orange tow float to my waist band and strap the electronic timing chip to the inside of my left ankle.

Swimmers are allocated to four waves, or categories, determined by their submitted finishing times, and I am allocated to the wave of green capped "novice" swimmers with the slowest times. My wave of green capped "novices" are transported by "Mountain Goat" minibus down the western length of the lake to the start of the race at Lake Bank, located in the south west of the lake (OS Grid Ref: SD290900).

Swimmers are a hardy and friendly bunch in the main and there is a real "buzz" as we await our pre-swim briefing at lake shore. Many have travelled from all over the country to take part. Most of my fellow "green caps" are wet suited but a few brave souls come "bare backed". Many have purposefully "Vaselined" their necks, arm pits and back of knees; it is a wise move and I later greatly regret that I didn't follow suit. "The water's 17 degrees C!" someone announces.

And as this is intended to be my last open water swim of the season I am determined to give it "my all". But I purposefully take heed of the pre start pep talk given by Colin Hill, director of "Chillswim" and race organiser, "It's a long way, so no adrenalin rushes" he insists. "Take your time and treat the first mile as a warm up".

Coniston Water is the third longest lake in Cumbria, and has been likened to a fjord for reasons of its exceptional depth and alignment, not to mention its stunning wooded hillside setting. The views from the bay are exceptional, revealing the true splendour of the lake, dominated by the iconic Old Man of Coniston.

And so for water! We start a little after 8:00am. Canoeists diligently cover our every move as we swim across the southern lake bay and head for the wooded, eastern shore. The young canoeist from the ubiquitous Carlisle Canoe Club chuckles as she explains that long strands of weeds are wrapped all around my neck....

Captain Webb might have swum the English Channel in 1875 using breaststroke but few would now champion the same stroke for open water swimming for reasons of the body's resistance to water and the strain that the stroke can put on the knees. And don't I know it! My initial progress is hampered by a stiff left knee, recently sprained in the course of inspecting bridges at work in the County, and I don't risk kicking "in anger" until I sight the yellow inflatable buoy marking the one mile distance.

Fortunately, any lingering pain soon passes. Rocks rise dramatically from either side as we squeeze through the narrow gorge twixt Peel Island and the south eastern shore. This is the land that inspired Arthur Ransome to write "Swallows and Amazons". But I had better beware. "Move over to the left!" warns a nearby canoeist, "Ouch!" Too late! I suddenly ground to an errant halt on top of a rock outcrop that leads far into the channel.

We swim approximately 50 metres off the eastern shore for most of the lake in near perfect conditions. The water is so wonderfully benign and the course is clearly marked out with yellow and red buoys at alternate half mile stages.

1.5 miles: The first feeding station, marked by a huge red inflatable buoy, consists of a small boat anchored just off Dales Wood Jetty. A handful of helpers are kept busy stretching over the gunwales and offering drinks of water and energy drink. Swimmers are not allowed to touch any feeding boat, for fear of capsizing their craft, and it takes a while to get the hang of downing the energy drink whilst leaning on the tow float and treading water.

The leading swimmer of the second wave of orange capped swimmers races past like a man possessed, closely followed by a fearsome retinue of orange capped freestylers.

2.5 miles: "The best race I've ever been on!" enthuses an exuberant orange capped swimmer at the second feeding station as I gulp down a handful of energy sustaining jelly babies. Certainly the race is carried out in the most agreeable circumstances of friendship and good nature. A slight twinge of cramp shoots through my left calf as I resume swimming.

We are soon joined by a mass of yellow capped sprinters from the third wave. There are as many women as men swimming freestyle, but only a precious handful of swimmers race breaststroke.

Of course Coniston Water is forever associated with Donald Campbell's disastrous attempt at breaking the world water speed record on the 4th January 1967. Grainy back and white images of his beloved "Bluebird" somersaulting disastrously are forever etched in my memory. Fate should have it that our race passes close to the site of his watery grave.

Three miles gone, and a Rubicon is passed! I have never swum this far ever before. They do say that there is no gain without the pain and I admit that I struggle to the 3.5 mile feeding station.

4 Miles: canoeists race to protect us from the large number of boats messing about the lake near Coniston. The iconic Gondola steam yacht potters about the far western bay inconsequentially, belching grey smoke out of its top hat high funnel, for good effect.

The first of the fourth and last wave of pink capped "elite" swimmers barges through the crowd of orange and yellow caps congregating about the final 4.5 mile feeding station to demand an energy drink. He is really fired up and swims "bare backed", for good measure!

I don't know what they put in the blackcurrant flavoured energy drink at the feeding station but it really helps me push the stroke! However, progress is halted once I stray into a dense patch of straggly weeds. Clumps of the blessed stuff literally wrap around everywhere and I am forced to use my arms to claw out a route. Fortunately it soon passes.

Eureka! I pass the 5 mile yellow buoy in a state of near ecstasy! Now I can sense victory. The swim finishes beside Monk Coniston Car Park, at the north eastern corner of the lake. I manage to summon enough residual energy to manufacture a decent racing breaststroke down the final 250 metres. Near chaos develops as swimmers converge from all directions and begin to wind up for a last, mad rush to the finishing point (OS Grid Ref: NY316977).

Good natured cheers and applause from a large crowd of onlookers greet every swimmer as we emerge from the water. My balance is gone and a hand is offered to steady me as I am told to step onto the finishing mat and handed a medal "for my efforts". I lean against a convenient crowd barrier much longer than is needed whilst a volunteer struggles to remove the electronic timer off my left ankle. I am delighted to have completed in a time of 4 hours 45 minutes and 07 seconds.

Slowly, I struggle over to the finish area, crowded with fellow swimmers, to retrieve my kit and struggle out of my shredded wet suit with the help of a willing volunteer. "Your neck is really chafed!" sighs a South African neighbour with genuine alarm. As though I really care!

This has been a wonderful experience, a celebration of all that's good about open water swimming and the Lake District. Some swims are memorable for all the wrong reasons but I doubt if conditions or the organisation, on the day, could be bettered. Yes, I may be tired; yes, I may be woozy, chafed and bloated from drinking far more lake water than is good for me, but that is scant inconvenience. It is time to catch the "Mountain Goat" minibus back to school for a well-earned shower and change.

PS The fastest swimmer was Dion Harrison (West Yorkshire) who finished in an impressive time of 1 hour 58 minutes and 10 seconds!

"OVER-WINTERING"

So what is a budding Open Water Swimmer supposed to do in the winter when the lakes become far too cold to endure, with or without a wet suit? Some hardy friends may look forward to taking the plunge in Windermere's annual "Big Chill Swim" extravaganza or even partake in New Year's Day swims in Whitehaven harbour. Alas, neither event appeals to me!

Come the October hour change and I am more than content to be heading down to my local authority pool in Carlisle, aka "The Pools", and churning out the lengths. Of course it is a shock to the system having to transfer from the glorious and near limitless freedom of the lakes with some of the most stunning backgrounds in England to the confines of a crowded 25m pool.

Nevertheless, I must admit that "The Pools" has become something of a second home and I'm pleased to say that members of staff and fellow swimmers have become firm friends over the years.

I've got into the habit of swimming on a Sunday morning with a group of elderly enthusiasts. Even though some of them will never see eighty again they are a glowing testament to the advantages of regular exercise and a real inspiration to other users of the pool.

Take my friend, Clarrie, for example. He's now over ninety years young and regularly swims several times a week in the main pool. I even persuaded the local paper to take a photo of him in the pool on his ninetieth birthday with his friends from the so-called Sunday morning swimmers.

My visits to the pool also provide me with an opportunity to maintain my motivation and improve my stroke. Faye, a lifeguard and part time teacher, warns me that I need to radically change my stroke if I want to successfully manage the really big lakes. She insists that I must quicken my laboured arm movements and purchase much more shoulder strength.

They do say that you can't teach old dogs new tricks. And rest assured I endure a couple of difficult months as I endure all sorts of problems, adapting to changes in balance, breathing and co-ordination. Practice eventually makes near perfect and I try out my new stroke in the annual "Swimathon" 5 kilometre sponsored charity swim held at Hexham pool in April 2015. And I'm delighted to find that I swim over five minutes quicker than my previous year's time. Now, all I need do is buy a new wet suit and hopefully I'll be ready for the summer!

YEAR TWO
FULL OF GOOD INTENTIONS

Full, of good intentions, I try and "kick start" the second season of lake swimming by working on the improved breaststroke, buying a new wet suit and even travelling down to Manchester to listen to Adam Walker tell of his extraordinary swimming adventures.

The recent growth and popularity of open water swimming has brought much needed publicity to a number of remarkable British swimmers who have achieved considerable fame in lakes and high seas over the last few years.

Take Adam Walker, for instance, who is the first Briton (and the sixth person in history) to swim the toughest seven oceans in the world. He recounted his extraordinary tale of hardship and achievement to an enthralled audience in Manchester.

Adam is a sobering demonstration of what mere mortals can achieve. He took seven years to complete his epic journey. This involved swimming all seven of the world's most difficult open water channels, or passages. These were the English Channel; the Straits of Gibraltar; the Molokai Channel, Hawaii; the Catalina Channel, USA; Tsugaru Channel, Japan; the Cook Strait, New Zealand; and finally the North Channel, between Northern Ireland and Scotland.

So what motivates Adam? He is keen to stress that he's a normal bloke and only became interested in open water swimming after watching a film on a plane, titled "On a Clear Day", which featured the story of an unemployed worker down on his luck who decides to take fate into his own hands and swim the English Channel.

Driven by an unrivalled will power that appears only matched by a near suicidal desperation to succeed at any cost, he recounts overcoming a near debilitating shoulder injury, never mind numerous bouts of seasickness and leg cramps. And that's not including having to contend with any number of marauding sharks, ocean swells and contrary currents, shoals of jelly fish, sea fog and freezing temperatures!

Although he may be keen to stress his mantra of "Pain lasts for a minute…. success lasts for a lifetime" he admits that the pain from being stung by a Portuguese Man of War on the Hawaiian leg of the journey was pure "torture". Enough said. Nevertheless, he was particularly keen to highlight moments of pure delight, especially when he was surrounded by an accompanying pod of twelve dolphins on the New Zealand leg of his journey.

It is no real surprise that Adam Walker should capture the imagination of an enraptured audience. After all, there is a long established tradition in Lancashire of celebrating swimming champions and treating them as public heroes.

The tradition goes back well over 150 years, to the beginnings of organised swimming competitions in England. Thousands would line the banks of the River Irwell or lake to see the stars compete. I am minded that a namesake, E.B.Mather, a professional swimmer from Manchester, was feted for becoming Champion of England in the 1860's. He gained this accolade for beating all comers in a 2 mile race down the River Thames on three separate occasions in 1862, 1863 and 1865. He gained a silver cup and 200 guineas for each of his achievements; this was not an inconsiderable prize, given that a Lancashire mill worker was lucky to be earning the equivalent of £1.50 a week at this time!

There were many others; most came from industrial northern towns and were equally adept at swimming in unheated municipal baths, moorland reservoirs and salt laden seas. Sadly, most of their names and achievements are long forgotten but a few enthusiasts are keen

to preserve the names and achievements of the likes of Chadderton's Henry Taylor who won 3 Gold Medals at the 1908 London Olympics and Salford's Mark Addy, a much vaunted lifesaver decorated by Queen Victoria for rescuing over 50 people from the River Irwell.

I make no apology for mentioning my recent efforts to resurrect the name of Trafford's Percy Courtman, a pre-First World War Olympic medallist and World Record breaststroke swimmer who was tragically killed in 1917 whilst serving his country in France.

And I wonder how many readers have previously heard of Joseph D. Foster, the Oldham swimmer who became the first man to swim the length of Windermere in 1911? "Joseph who?" I hear you exclaim. Precisely...

Fortunately, Great Britain continues to "churn out" a considerable number of champion swimmers who are wonderful ambassadors for the sport. Take Keri-anne Payne and Cassie Patten, for example. These wonderful role models won very creditable silver and bronze medals, respectively, at the inaugural Womens' 10 kilometre swim in the 2008 Beijing Olympics. They both represented Stockport Metro Swimming Club at the time.

There are many others. I am particularly proud of having met Duncan Goodhew, Olympic Champion and President of the "Swimathon" charity, when he journeyed up to the pools in Carlisle several years ago to thank charity swimmers for their efforts.

But I have to leave the last word and "bragging rights" to my friend Beth who can boast having a cup of coffee in a swanky upmarket Cheshire restaurant with double Olympic Gold medallist Becky Adlington a few years ago!

"Did you tell her about my swimming book*?" pleaded I, as she later recounted her chance encounter on the phone.

"No!" she demurred....

*"Illustrated Guide to Greater Manchester's Public Swimming Pools" (ISBN: 978-1-291-11790-5)

RESERVOIRS AND RESTRICTIONS

It is time I resume my Open Water Challenge. Regrettably, it comes as a shock to discover that I can only swim in three of the six lakes that I plan to "tick off" this summer. And the reason is quite simple; the other three lakes that I have selected, Haweswater, Thirlmere and Ennerdale Water, are all reservoirs and the current owners, United Utilities, do not permit swimming in any of their waters.

I contacted United Utilities' Head Office to clarify the situation and the Company responded by sending me documents which stated that their policy has been introduced in the light of their statutory Health and Safety obligations to the general public who visit their reservoirs and catchment areas. They stated that there is the need for a clear unambiguous message to the public at large of the consequences and dangers of swimming in reservoirs, and added that their main focus of their strategy is focussed on education and "communication-awareness" of the dangers of swimming in reservoirs.

They also supplied me with a fact sheet which warns of the dangers and nasty illnesses that you can pick up while swimming in untreated open water "such as a reservoir". The list includes, and I quote, such "nasties" as eye infections (trachoma); parasitic diseases (cryptosporidium); worm eggs (whipworm) and Weils disease. Well, all I can say is heaven help the unsuspecting recipients of admittedly treated water at the other end of the tap, never mind the occasional illegal swimmer, if that is what your average reservoir contains!!!!!

It's sobering to realise that issues concerning reservoirs and the Lake District are nothing new. The region has suffered from the harmful effects of mining and industry for centuries, never mind unwelcome railway and road builds. And, not surprisingly, Manchester Corporation's controversial plan to construct Thirlmere reservoir in the 1890s achieved national prominence and even created one of the first ever environmental protection movements in the world. But more of that later.

It is more than likely that the Lake District will continue to face further and more complex environmental challenges. And here is not the place to discuss the implications of climate change being a potential "game changer".

Of course I am disappointed with the United Utilities response. Nevertheless, I feel that I should still include all three reservoirs within my challenge, if only to make readers aware of their controversial history and realise the environmental battles that have endured within the Lake District.

And so reluctantly I decide to try and make the best of all three "forbidden" lakes by attempting to either walk around their shores or even investigating the possibility of putting a boat on their waters.

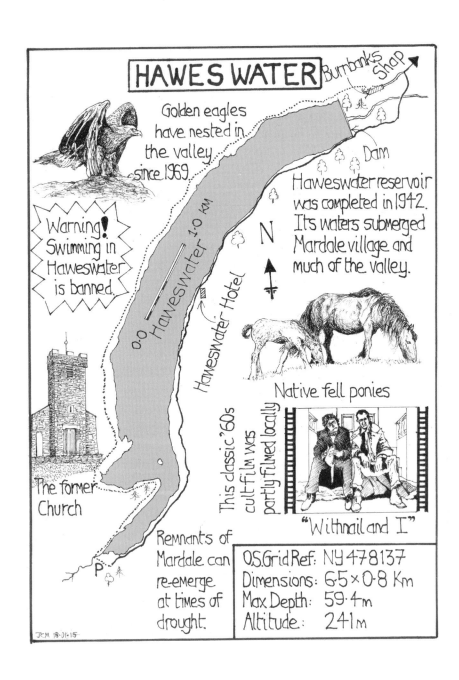

HAWES WATER

Burnbanks Shop

Golden eagles have nested in the valley since 1969.

Warning! Swimming in Haweswater is banned.

Haweswater 1.0 KM   0.0

Dam

Haweswater reservoir was completed in 1942. Its waters submerged Mardale village and much of the valley.

N

Haweswater Hotel

Native fell ponies

The former Church

This classic '60s cult film was partly filmed locally

"Withnail and I"

Remnants of Mardale can re-emerge at times of drought.

P

O.S. Grid Ref:	NY 478 137
Dimensions:	6.5 × 0.8 Km
Max Depth:	59.4 m
Altitude:	241 m

JCM 18·01·15

HAWESWATER (7/17)

Thursday 23 April 2015

I turn my attention to visiting Haweswater. It is huge by any standards, over 4 miles long and 0.5 miles wide. Not that it is easy to reach. It lies in the heart of the one of the most lonely and least accessible tracts of fell land in the whole of the Lake District, which also happens to be the sacred haunt of deer herd and fell pony.

It has also proved to be one of the most contentious and controversial waters in the Lake District, as a result of Manchester Water Corporation's controversial decision in 1919 to construct a reservoir on the site of two smaller lakes existing in the valley. This resulted in the construction of a 30 metre high dam wall; the raising of the water level and flooding of much of the upper valley and submerging of the existing village of Mardale.

United Utilities, the current owners of the reservoir, may boast that this is the biggest reservoir in the north west of England, easily dwarfing Thirlmere, but the fact remains that access to the water is pathetic for leisure users.

Even though Haweswater is the only significant stretch of water in the Lake District that neither permits boating nor swimming, I feel that I should include the lake in my challenge, if only to make readers aware of its controversial history and the restrictions on swimming.

And so, despite my keenness to resume my mission to swim in all the big 17 lakes, I am reduced to following the perimeter or the lake, as best I can by "shanks's pony", albeit as close to the shoreline as protective stone wall or wire fence will allow!

I start my walk in the remote hamlet of Burnbanks, nestling in the wooded shelter of the huge dam wall. How curious then, given the very obvious restrictions, that a road side information board should state that: "…Lake District water is a precious commodity: it moulds the local landscape, supports agriculture, and encourages sport and tourism…"

What a glorious morning to be walking the fells! The sun shines and bird song is prolific. It has been a long winter. And even though stubborn wisps of frozen snow are clinging desperately by their finger nails to reluctant ridge tops, spring is definitely in the air in the valley with fresh born lambs a jumping and trees a budding.

I follow the shore path along the northern edge of the lake. So still, the lake's vast surface reflects a glorious enamel blue. Senses are heightened by the gushing roar of fell stream plunging down to some hidden ice cold pool guarded by yellow gorse.

There are some wonderful moments to cherish, not least chancing upon the unmistakable blur of red squirrel darting up the dry stone wall surrounding an abandoned farmstead, shielded by coniferous plantation.

And not to mention the "staccato" of woodpecker busily drilling high up a towering pine; the distinctive flight of blackened cormorant with neck outstretched as it skims low over the water surface and the raucous croak of rooks encircling a nearby craggy summit.

Is there no end of the signs proclaiming that Haweswater holds up to 84 billion litres of water and daily supplies a quarter of all the North West's drinking water? It's all very impressive, I'm sure, but the fact remains that at times of water draw-down, a wide gleaming white band encircles much of the shore line. Norman Nicholson, the late, great Millom poet, described this woeful apparition so wonderfully when he said that it resembled a line of swimming pool tiles!

So follows an intriguing couple of miles wandering around the indented south western corner of the lake, overseen by some serious and remote mountain ridges. What a blessed racket those geese make! They seem to occupy every bay in the lake shore and advertise their noisy presence with a violent outburst of aggressive honking, ad nauseam. Regrettably, Riggindale's lofty ramparts can no longer hold bragging rights for hosting England's last surviving nesting golden eagle.....

The near shoreline bears testament to the lost hamlet of Mardale, submerged when the reservoir was flooded. Remnants of the village habitually re-appear when water levels drop in summer droughts.

Yet another information board, warning the unwary that the water temperature in the reservoir is rarely above freezing, greets me as I round the crowded car park at the southern end of the lake. That is obviously good news for the native population of the elusive schelly fish which occupy the lake's lower regions, but bad news for anyone foolhardy enough to attempt an illegal swim.

Regrettably, several sections of the following shoreline path are closed and I am forced to complete the second half of my circuit by lakeside road. Admittedly, views are quite spectacular and it gives me an opportunity to stop for refreshments in the Haweswater Hotel.

Built at the time of the reservoir, and intended to replace the ancient Dun Bull Inn, it sports some choice Art Deco facilities and considerable memorabilia of what life must have been life pre-reservoir. I drink a pot of tea and consume a huge wedge of carrot cake in a deserted bar under the watchful-or, is it bemused?-gaze of the head of a deer stag mounted on the adjoining wall.

A caption explains how this unfortunate stag, which goes by the name of "The Mardale Stag", was killed near the hotel and that its head was presented by the wife of the late Alderman Isaac Hinchcliffe in 1937. How times have changed! Could you dare imagine the outcry if someone took a pot shot at a prize stag these days?

The road continues past the dam wall before a path leads through wooded slope. I return to Burnbanks for mid-afternoon.

I appreciate that United Utilities have to safeguard their water and public safety but the sad fact remains that the lack of recreation facilities is shameful.

RYDAL WATER REVISITED

Wednesday 27 May 2015

What a wet and windy evening to be swimming in Rydal Water! It is such an unpromising start for our inaugural swim of the year. There is method in our madness; after all, it's acknowledged that Rydal Water is one of the first lakes to warm up. Rain falls heavily as we change on the shingle beach at Steps End.

The water seems surprisingly agreeable as I take my first tentative steps. At least, I am in good company. Jordan is a triathlete of some stature, having recently represented Great Britain in the European youth team championship and won a bronze for his efforts. And soon he and his dad, Kevin, are going through their paces with some determined sprinting to the northern shore boat house and back.

Matt admits that he has not swum for over a year, well before he served with the Royal Engineers in Afghanistan, and is keen to accompany me on an anti-clockwise circuit around Heron Island. We take it slowly.

Summits are obscured by a ghostly veil of incessant rain cloud. And yet, despite the rain, there is something undoubtedly mystical and enthralling about swimming in this lake; the water is so pure and captivating. Swifts flit magically hither and thither bounding with joie de vivre just above the water's surface.

We are very much on our own, making silent passage; curiosity compels us to circuit an additional rocky outcrop beyond. A sudden wind rises, unsettling these normally even calm waters unpleasantly, as we head for home. We follow the southern shore, flanked by carpets of bluebell tumbling down to water's edge.

My left leg cramps viciously as I struggle to regain the sloping beach; both feet have long been leaden and I struggle back to change. I'm desperate to take off my wet suit and pile on the clothes whilst I shiver near dementedly. And to think that the lake registered a barely credible 14 degrees centigrade during April's warm spell!

So follows a pleasant half hour or so in the comforts of the adjoining "Badger Bar". There's opportunity for Jordan to tell us some of his exploits of triathleting in Ukraine and some of the unsavoury perils of his rivals' antics...

Despite the appalling weather, everyone agrees that this has been a great swim.

BROTHERS WATER

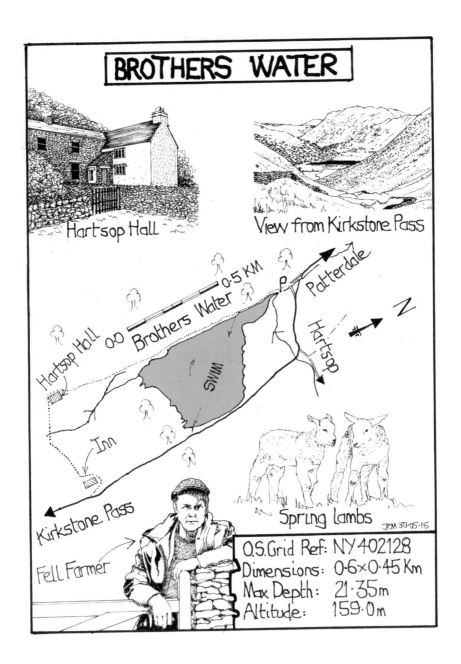

Hartsop Hall

View from Kirkstone Pass

Hartsop Hall
0·0 Brothers Water
0·5 KM
SWIM
P
Patterdale
Hartsop
N
Inn
Kirkstone Pass
Fell Farmer
Spring lambs
JRM 30·05·15

O.S.Grid Ref: NY 402128
Dimensions: 0·6×0·45 Km
Max Depth: 21·35m
Altitude: 159·0m

BROTHERS WATER (8/17)

Friday 19 June 2015

What a disappointing summer! Unfortunately the lakes just aren't warming up and our intrepid band of open water swimmers have to make do with freezing water temperatures as best we can. We still take the opportunity to swim across Brothers Water one Friday afternoon.

Brothers Water occupies a dramatic location, squeezed into the narrow head of Patterdale valley, between the near endless length of Ullswater and the foot of the perilous Kirkstone Pass. Roughly circular in plan and barely 500 metres long, Brothers Water may be the smallest of the 17 so-called Big Lakes but it punches well above its weight for impressive views and dramatic effect. And, more importantly, it offers a cracking swim.

At least it's dry as we park at Cow Bridge Car Park (OS Grid Ref: NY402134) and take the short stroll up a tree lined path beside the fleet flowing Goldrill Beck to the northern tip of the lake. A convenient shingle beach provides ideal shelter to change (OS Grid Ref: NY402130).

I'm pleased that we continue to attract new blood, and Ben has joined regulars Tom, Adam, Jordan and myself for the swim. Ben might be well regarded as a local club cricketer and rugby union player, but he still manages to put his wet suit on "back to front!!

At least I am having better luck putting on my brand new "Blue 70" wet suit; I am really looking forward to using it "in anger" for the very first time. I'm pleased that I bought it from "Swim the Lakes" in Ambleside because the store comes highly recommended for advising and supplying swimmers with good equipment.

And true to form, Sarah, the assistant and very enthusiastic swimmer, selected a couple of Blue 70 "Sprint" wetsuits for me to try on. Although the first felt slightly tight the second one fitted like the proverbial glove. As well as feeling oh so light around the shoulders and neck, she explained that this particular suit is fabricated so as not to be too buoyant in the legs. This is obviously appropriate for "breaststroke legs". And it peels off wonderfully! (Obviously the store also stocks lots and lots of other Blue 70 "Sprint" wetsuits suitable for free-style swimmers.)

Any good natured banter is quickly curtailed when Tom notices a broken glass beer bottle protruding from water's edge. The prospect of any one of us stepping on its jagged edges just does not bear thinking about. A quick sweep of our beach reveals yet more debris and signs of an illegal camp fire. Why, oh why, I ask do some people want to damage something so beautiful and magical?

So here goes! Carefully avoiding any number of large stones littering the lake edge we quickly enter the water. And it is cold enough to instantaneously numb my feet as I kick out from shore. Guide books may state that the lake is 17 metres deep but we quickly discover that the shallow edges extend at least 50 metres out into the lake. Trust Tom to delight in continually standing up just to show how shallow the lake really is!

Temperatures are not helped by an unwelcome breeze that disturbs the surface annoyingly. Once we gain deep water, our party fragments with Tom and Jordan forging well ahead with me in tow. Wisely, Ben and Adam make cautious progress to the rear.

Our original plan to circuit the lake isn't practical, bearing in mind those extensive shallow edges and instead we decide to head right across the centre of the lake towards the far south eastern bay. This will also ensure that we don't disturb that pair of resident swans cruising about the extensive reed beds littering the southern shore.

It proves an inspired choice. There is something wonderfully satisfying about swimming in remote lakes and being so close to nature. This is a majestic landscape. It is hard to do full justice to the views from the centre of the lake; we appear to inhabit the centre of a natural amphitheatre with stark green fell sides plummeting down to a densely wooded shoreline.

Legend states that the lake was originally known as Broad Water and the name was changed to Brothers Water to commemorate the drowning of two brothers. It is difficult to know when fact becomes legend with some Lakeland folklore, although William Wordsworth mentioned such an event occurring in 1785. The brothers were apparently skating on the frozen lake in the winter when they fell through the ice.

The water remains wonderfully clear and deep all the way to the far shore. Trust Jordan to sprint ahead and already be stepping out on to shore well ahead as Tom and I pass a large clump of yellow blooming water lilies growing in the sheltered bay; they are as unexpected as picturesque.

It is still cold enough to discourage Tom, Jordan and me from lingering at lake edge any longer than is absolutely necessary. And as soon as we check that Ben and Adam are alright, we return "to base" by a longer dog leg of a route.

What a co-incidence that the sun should finally shine as we race for home! Jordan fast sprints the final 200 metres in a most impressive frenzy of whirring arms and powerful leg kicks.

It proves a lovely early evening. And improving conditions allow us to change at a leisurely pace and chat about the swim. It is satisfying to know that we've all swum well over a kilometre in not much more than 30 minutes.

P.S. The National Trust owns the lake and clearly does not allow any boating. I phoned the National Trust's Grasmere Offices before our swim to clarify if I needed their permission to swim in the lake. "Not sure," came the reply. Despite taking my number and promising that "someone will ring you back," no one did.

I can only suggest that swimmers seek clarification from the National Trust on this matter before they consider swimming in the lake.

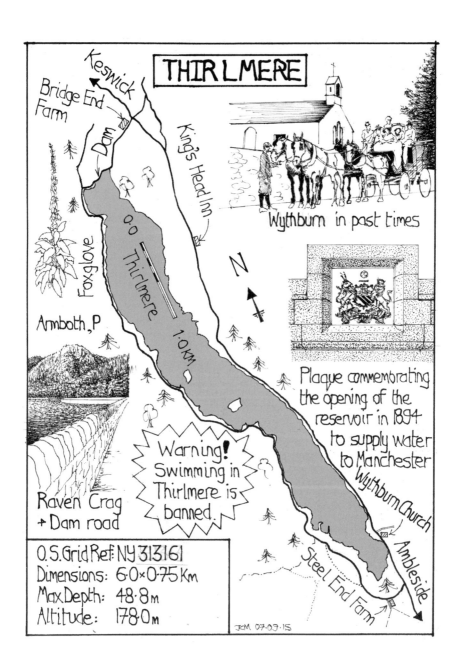

THIRLMERE

Keswick

Bridge End Farm

Dam

King's Head Inn

0.0

Thirlmere

1.0 KM

N

Foxglove

Armboth P

Wythburn in past times

Plaque commemorating the opening of the reservoir in 1894 to supply water to Manchester

Wythburn Church

Ambleside

Raven Crag + Dam road

Warning! Swimming in Thirlmere is banned.

Steel End Farm

O.S. Grid Ref: NY 313161
Dimensions: 6.0 × 0.75 Km
Max Depth: 48.8 m
Altitude: 178.0 m

JcM 07.09.15

THIRLMERE (9/17)

Wednesday 01 July 2015

At long last, high pressures and warm sunny skies are the order of the day! Is it any wonder that I should seize the opportunity and head for Thirlmere? Reservoirs in the Lake District are an emotive issue at the best of times. And Thirlmere is the oldest, and it has to be said most controversial, reservoir in the entire Lake District.

Although I cannot swim in its waters I discover that I can at least explore its waters by row boat. And after pitching my tent at Bridge End Farm, located at the northern end of the lake (01768-772166), I head out for the lake, despite a fellow camper warning me that "it looks a bit choppy!"

Thirlmere is quite an enigmatic lake. It was built out of necessity, to supply drinking water to the citizens of Victorian Manchester in 1894, at a desperate time of insanitation, epidemic and thirst in the city. Despite being four miles in length, it is largely hidden from public view by dense vegetation and visitors are few in numbers despite the authorities' best attempts to allow some limited use.

I have previously spoken to United Utilities, care of the Northern Catchment Team, The Old Sawmill, Thirlmere (01768-772334) regarding permission "to float my boat". I was advised that I can launch from Armboth Car Park, located a mile or so down a narrow winding forest road on the western "other" side of the reservoir (OS Grid Ref: NY306172).

NB Engine craft are not allowed on the lake. (For a princely sum you can park for 24 hours, use the toilets and read lots and lots of information boards and signs warning of the perils of swimming!)

It is quite a foreboding place. And I am keen to detach the boat from the trailer and wheel it down a steep rough and broken gravel track leading down to the shore line as quickly as I can! A quick inspection reveals that that the water in the near bay to be quite calm, which is good news.

I always associate small boats with the Lake District in the same way that cycles are ridden in Amsterdam and Kendal Mint Cake has to be taken on Everest expeditions. The two should be inseparable but reality proves otherwise. There seems to be few small boats available bearing in mind the eligible surface area on offer. More's the pity. Because I cannot think of any finer way of spending a hot summer's day than rowing a leisurely hour or so on gentle waters "far from the madding crowd".

Needless to say, there aren't any other boaters about. And yet my activities soon attract a number of interested onlookers who congregate at water's edge and watch me launch.

Pushing out the boat into deep water, whilst trying to jump on and grabbing the timber oars to ensure that they don't slip out of their rowlocks at the same time, is easier said than done! I am finally on the water for 2:30pm. It is quite a while since I last rowed the boat "in anger" and I am having to quickly reacquaint myself with handling the boat in the sheltered bay adjoining the launch spot.

I intend to complete an anti-clockwise eight mile long circuit of the lake and so begin by heading southwards. Venturing out of the confines of the bay into the lake proper provides me with an unwelcome invitation into waters agitated by a brisk southerly wind.

So follows a tough ten minute assignment and I quickly learn that it is wise to cling close to the densely tree lined shoreline and keep one eye scanned for suitable landing sites "just in case". But it is patently obvious that there just aren't any! (Worst luck).

Waves continue to lap the craft noisily and one or two even manage to break over the gunwales. Once I manage to head into the lee of Deergarth How Island, the most northerly of the two dollops of wooded islands close to the western shore, I can start to relax and take a breather! Now I can begin to enjoy my journey and marvel at the remarkable view of Helvellyn's humped back form looming over to the east.

Thirlmere reservoir dates from 1894 when St John's Beck was dammed, the existing waters were more than doubled in area and their level raised by 50 feet. Of course it wasn't always like this. Before the reservoir came,

Thirlmere valley appeared the very epitome of a rural idyll, complete with two small lakes, 2 villages and 14 farms with roots traced back to Viking times. William Wordsworth often met his friend and fellow poet, Robert Southey at Wythburn's Cherry Tree Inn and his observations of the locals "at play" making merry with dancing and festivities are joyfully recorded in "The Travellers".

Myths and legends haunt the valley from days gone by. These involve black dogs reputed to swim the lake, chiming bells, fiery lights and maidens drowning on their wedding nights. And the former Armboth House was regarded as the most haunted house in Cumberland!

I soon settle into pleasant routine. The boat rides high and handles well and my arms are pulling the oars deep and strongly. It takes an hour's steady rowing to pass Hawes Howe Island, the second of the two wooded dollops, to regain open water. Distances are immense and I now realise there is still a long way to go. So follows quite a busy few minutes as I round the exposed headland about Hause Point and find myself battling yet more irritated waters.

Naturally, I steer back to the relative safety of the western shore as soon as possible, as I continue to take on yet more water from overlapping waves…

It was no wonder that Manchester's plans for the construction of a reservoir at Thirlmere met fierce opposition and inspired one of the first environmental struggles of modern times. Influential opponents, including John Ruskin and Thomas Carlyle, formed the Thirlmere Defence Association (TDA) in 1877. The plans developed into a "battle royal" between the authorities in Manchester, desperate for clean water, healthy sanitation and epidemic free streets, and conservationists who argued passionately about the need to preserve Thirlmere in its "wild" form.

Such was the depth of feeling for the preservation of Thirlmere that Manchester's plans had to be submitted 11 times through Parliament before they were finally given Royal Assent by Queen Victoria on 23th May 1879. And the rest as they say is history.

It's quite a relief to stop rowing and be able to rest awhile in the sheltered bay at Dubgill Bridge and let the boat drift ever so slowly southwards. It also gives me opportunity to bail out amidships! So follows a pleasant thirty minutes rowing in the gentle sheltered waters of Wythburn Bay leading to the shallow waters of the southern end of the lake.

Masses of Canada geese feed noisily close to shore as I turn the boat round at the southern end of the lake and head back to mid lake. I make good progress, aided by the strength of a prevailing wind. There is something enormously satisfying and strangely reassuring about being on the water and even the odd, short rain storm can't dent my enthusiasm. It only takes 30 minutes to regain Hawes Howe Island; nearby an unmarked rock plays host to a legion of screeching gulls.

Of course construction was vital to ensure that Manchester maintained a water supply and there is no doubting the genius of the dam construction and the ingenuity in the way that waters are conveyed to Manchester by way of a 95 mile long gravity aqueduct.

Thirlmere's magnificent Victorian engineering cannot be totally disguised by all those massed ranks of trees and it is regrettable that Manchester Corporation chose to build prominent features, like the draw off tower, in a mock baronial style. Sturdy, yes, but hardly in keeping with the locale. Many consider that the valley has paid a heavy price for Manchester's insatiable thirst and feel that its legacy has left a nasty stain on the Lake District that can never be removed.

Sadly, only a handful of historical buildings survived the building of the reservoir. These include "lowly" Wythburn Chapel, constructed in 1640 and Dalehead House, the ancient Manor Hall of the Leathes family. And ironically, it has also served as the summer holiday home of the Mayor of Manchester and as a luxury hotel!

Wary of approaching too closely those natural rock protuberances, that could all too easily ground my boat at the dam wall, I turn round and make a final "charge" to Armboth shoreline a little after 6pm. Pity about all those swarms of midges waiting to meet and greet me as I strip down the boat and drive back to the campsite for a well-earned meal!

EPIC EVENTS

And so this wretched summer continues to disappoint! What a shame for anyone wanting to camp, never mind open water swim, in the Lake District. Regrettably, I am struggling to find a boat crew to support my end to end Derwent Water Swim, so I offer to help marshal the "Epic Events" swim at Derwent Water in the meantime.

"Epic Events" provides a very popular annual series of enjoyable swims in Derwent Water, Ullswater and Coniston Water; competitors can select one of three separate distances which are classified as Iron Man (3.8km), Intermediate (1 mile) or Novice (500m).

Obviously, the prospect of a free swim, "T" shirt and bacon butty helps but I had not realised how much there was to do before the swims can start! Jo McWilliams, the enthusiastic Race Director, greets all the assembled volunteers warmly as we begin to set up the Event HQ for starters. It's a well-practised routine and many hands definitely make light work of erecting gazebos and whatever.

I appreciate that not everyone would enjoy lugging "portable" electrical generators down to the lake shore at 6:30am but we also have to set up the Start/Finish pen for the swimmers at water's edge. Time is critical and we all pitch  in, erecting yet more gazebos, positioning the inflatable starter gate and timing mats at water's edge and erecting yards and yards of crowd barrier to help corral the swimmers.

People are friendly and I'm really pleased to meet up with three other marshals from my "neck of the woods": Nina, Rachel and Rosie. Their enthusiasm for swimming is infectious and laughter erupts when Chris

Kitchin's roll call is interrupted by an impromptu test of the powerful sound system blasting across the waters....

We are all given roles for the day, be it registering swimmers, handing out the electronic timing chips and medals, first aid or, whatever. I am assigned the role of "bio sprayer" on all three swims. This means that I'm responsible for spraying down all the swimmers' wet suits after they have finished the race and exiting the finish pen. Finishers arrive in a steady trickle and patiently wait to be hosed down. Everyone is so patient and good natured as they wait their turn to be sprayed. "How much do you have to pay to wash down women?" teases one woman competitor!

This is not a mere precaution but a safeguard to prevent the spread of invasive non-native species (INNS). All swimmers are urged to take time and care to check, clean and dry their swimming kit thoroughly before and after swimming and remove any plant matter or aquatic life that may have attached themselves.

The event attracts a large number of competitors and a surprising range of ages and abilities. You've got to hand it to those two competitors who arrive on wheel chairs but still manage to swim successfully around the course! Of course the swimmers' safety is paramount and both safety boats and kayakers patrol the course. In addition, the number of swimmers entering and leaving the race is recorded in triplicate.

I enjoy listening to swimmers telling me why they want to compete. I admire Paul for wanting to swim the one mile race in an attempt to regain his fitness after breaking a leg whilst playing Rugby League in Wigan. But the proudest person on the day must be that 77 year old lady who completes the 500m course despite having only learnt to swim at the ripe old age of 67 years!

I must be a glutton for punishment because I also offer to marshal at the subsequent "Epic Events" swim which is held in Coniston Water. As well as "bio-spraying" finishers from two of the races I compete in the one mile race.

Competitors are split into three separate "waves" which are distinguished by different colours of caps, orange, green and pink. Despite my best intentions to avoid trouble, I still end up with a painful crack on my toes in the habitual start of whirring arms and frantic leg kicks. So much for the aesthete who once described swimming as a sensuous pleasure! No matter, I soon get into my stride and find myself powering around the course. On days like these, you don't need to fight the water. You just harness its energy and go with the flow.

The swim rounds the four unequal sides of a course marked by huge inflatable yellow buoys. On passing the final buoy, I still have sufficient energy left "to press the accelerator" and pick off a handful of freestylers tiring on the approaches to the finishing gate. Job done! I am delighted to have completed the course in 39 minutes 45.8s. I am the 208th finisher of 284 starters.

Talk about no rest for the wicked! No sooner have I stripped off and changed back than I am soon helping lug equipment to the road end and loading it back into the Epic Event "Transits"....

DERWENT WATER

Penrith

Keswick

Grasmere

N

Boat Hire

SWIM

0.0
Derwent Water
1.0 KM

SWIM

Honister

JCM 22:12:15

The Moot Hall, Keswick

The Water is ideal for all aqua sports

Rowing boats for hire...

Herdwick Sheep

O.S. Grid Ref:	NY260211
Dimensions:	4·6×1·9 Km
Max Depth:	22·0 m
Altitude:	74·4 m

The rare Vendace fish is native to Derwent Water

DERWENT WATER (10/17)

Sunday 20 September 2015

Derwent Water is one of my favourite lakes, and I believe that it is seen at its very best in the autumn, when its wooded shoreline seems to glow with a bewildering array of rustic shades.

I am grateful to Dave C. for offering to accompany me on the swim in a rowboat. It's a great idea, and luck would have it that both Martin and Craig are both willing and available to help complete the crew.

My journey starts in the popular tourist town of Keswick. Conditions are promising as we arrive on the lake foreshore early Sunday morning. Pre-breakfast swimmers are already exiting from an energetic circuit of the near island as I struggle into my wet suit and kit up. The water temperature is predicted to be a pleasant 14 degrees Centigrade and a south westerly is expected to be blowing at an estimated 9mph.

The proprietors of the Keswick Launch Company (017687-72263), located at lake shore beside the "Theatre by the Lake", are keen to support my challenge and provide a lovely 4 man timber built row boat for the full day. It is a real beauty and we keenly climb aboard and hoist up my home made "Alpha" blue and white pennant to warn other craft of my swim. NB Boats are not available to support swimmers in July or August, their busiest months.

The crew take advantage of "flat calm" waters to familiarise themselves with the boat. We round the wooded head beyond the boat yard in Isthmus Bay and approach our start point situated on the public access shore (OS Grid Ref: NY258229). It's as far as we can row, as the rest of the northern shore is privately owned. Oars are fettered as the boat drifts ever so slowly to shore and halts with a gentle nudge onto the shingle beach.

"Don't tip us over!" warns Dave C as I motion to step onto the bow and jump onto dry land. It is now 10:00am and time to don my swimming cap and goggles and wade out into the bay's agreeably warm waters. There is something magical about plunging into new, unexplored waters and starting to swim, no matter how tentative my first strokes may be.

Of course first appearances can all too easily prove deceptive. And sure enough I learn, only too quickly, that conditions will become more "challenging" as the journey progresses. Despite a mysteriously "frozen" left shoulder and stiff neck, I soon break into a racing breaststroke.

The lake is shallow and oval in shape, three miles long and one mile wide and features an intricate shoreline and numerous islands. Ours is a straightforward route and I intend to head directly for the distant, grey stone built Lodore Falls Hotel standing proud of the far south eastern lake shore.

I quickly pass by Derwent Isle. Everything is so still and quiet, broken only by the agreeable laughter and chatter from my colleagues in the boat. It's a great and novel feeling to be accompanied by our wooded rowing boat. Effortlessly, the crew cleave a clean passage through rising waves. Always its presence is so reassuring. Sometimes our lines appear to merge but as quickly drift away.

So far so good! Thirty minutes into my journey and I espy Lords Isle somewhere to my distant left.

"You're doing really well, mate!" reassures Dave C. He is as generous in his praise as quick witted, a gentle giant from Enniskillen who quickly takes charge of the boat. He was once regarded as a very promising Rugby Union player in Carlisle's first team.

Steadily, but surely, the condition of the lake changes as I continue southwards; water temperatures are dropping markedly and waves, driven by a persistent south westerly, are rising. Vainly the sun tries to break through dense cloud mass without success. I swallow more than my fair share of water as I struggle to weather some quite choppy conditions in the next hour or so. All I can do is "dig deep" and hold my stroke. At least all this effort appears to have unlocked the frozen left shoulder!

I welcome a brief halt and sup of an energy drink, in the lee of St Herbert's Isle, that distinctive tree lined hump back located plumb centre of the lake.

Talk about being surrounded by "nature" in the raw! The Isle is named after Herbert, a 7th Century pilgrim and hermit who lived on the isle in solitude and was a close friend of St Cuthbert of Lindisfarne fame.

All large bodies of water seem to hold a secret or two. And Derwent Water is famous for being one of the last remaining habitats of the vendace (Coregonus vandesius), one of the rarest freshwater fishes to be found in the United Kingdom. Similar to the herring in appearance, it is distinctly marked with a blue, grey upper body and silvery white lower body. It grows to about 8" (200mm) in length.

Conditions deteriorate in the southern exposed half of the lake and I get a quite a battering from a seemingly endless pounding of waves. Desperately, I try to time each stroke to meet a lull in the next wave before waiting to be swamped by the next rush of water. At times like these I have to force myself to count each laboured stroke, to fight away any lingering self-doubts and concentrate my resolve. Suddenly, I am redirected to avoid a ridge line of protruding rocks, red buoy marked.

Maybe it is the location, or maybe the excitement of the swim, but I am suddenly reminded of the time I cross country skied with Cate up Newlands Valley, the other side of Cat Bells many more years ago than I dare to admit. What wonderful memories that trip still evokes of "ploughing" across freshly laid snow. We seemed to have the whole valley to ourselves....

Anyway, back to the job in hand. Imagine my relief to finally gain the sheltered and becalmed waters of the south western part of the lake. Sadly, there's hardly time to snatch a brief rest and gobble down half a banana to provide some energy for the final half mile, let alone opportunity to take in the spectacular views of tree lined cliffs towering above the near shore line. Whilst most of the lake appears devoid of other craft, the ever popular Kettlewell Bay sports a group of kayakers and wind surfers.

"You're on the last furlong," encourages Craig.

Experienced open water swimmers will tell you that the lakes are generally at their warmest in September. But they probably hadn't bargained for swimming in these shallow waters discharging directly off Scafell Pike and associated uplands! Yes, they are cold! I later discover that I cause the crew quite a scare when I apparently disappear underwater as I attempt to readjust the portion of wet suit chafing the back of my left knee. Fortunately, a worrying spasm of cramp in the right foot clears once I start to wriggle the offending object vigorously.

I am genuinely shocked by the amount of New Zealand pigmyweed (crassula helmsii) affecting this stretch of shore. I know that I have already written extensively about its existence but I had not expected that strands of the blessed stuff would even wrap themselves around the oars of the boat! All goes well until we almost run aground in extensive shallows of sand and silty mud!

But where to land? Boaters are warned to avoid the extensive wetlands surrounding the southern lake as they provide an important breeding habitat for snipe and the common sandpiper as well as a winter haven for wild fowl.

Instead, I decide to land beside the Keswick Launch jetty leading to the Lodore Falls Hotel, situated next to the "Great Bay". (NB. I have previously been given permission to land on this length of private shore by both the Keswick Launch Company and the adjoining "Platty Plus" Water Sports Centre.)

Timing is all important and I sense the crew's urgency as they hurry to enter the deep water channel "between launches". I struggle to keep up as the boat plunges into the narrow reed lined creek beyond, passing a couple of disinterested swans in the process. The scene is almost reminiscent of a setting straight out of a "Swallows and Amazons" storyline; the scatter of vivid red sea kayaks and row boats littering the deserted foreshore makes the illusion complete.

A few onlookers, awaiting the next ferry, watch intrigued as the crew cheer and applaud as I stroke the last few vital metres of water and struggle a few unsteady steps up the shingle beach onto dry land. It is far enough. (OS Grid Ref: NY265192).

We tie up on a convenient a pontoon for small boats beside the spindly launch jetty. It is now 12:10pm and I estimate that I've swum 2.75 miles in 2 hours 10 minutes. It's time to wolf down the remaining half of a banana and a handful of jelly beans, generously supplied by Dave C. They are widely recommended for giving the tired body a much needed boost.

Obviously I am delighted to have "ticked off" yet another lake and it is really nice of the owners of the "Platty Plus" Water Sports Centre to invite me to change in their facilities. All we now need to do is row back to the Keswick stage and have a celebratory pot of tea and toasted sandwiches!

ENNERDALE WATER

Ennerdale Bridge

River Ehen

P

Warning! Swimming in the lake is banned.

Angler's Crag

Lake View

N

0.0

Ennerdale Water

1.0 KM

P

Cormorant

JCM 17·02·16

The former USA President Bill Clinton proposed to Hillary on these lake shores in 1973!

O.S. Grid Ref: NY 107 14·9
Dimensions: 4·0 × 1·3 Km
Max Depth: 45·0 m
Altitude: 112·2 m

Black Sail Youth Hostel

R. Liza

ENNERDALE WATER (11/17)

Friday, 02 October 2015

Lake District weather is notorious for being fickle at the best of times. And I purposefully take advantage of a glorious and sustained Indian summer to put the boat on Ennerdale Water, the most westerly lake within the National Park.

It lies within Ennerdale Valley, one of the remotest valleys in the Lake District. This is wild country, well off the normal beaten track; facilities are non-existent and the valley does not even have a public road running its full length!

Ennerdale Water is a deep, glacial lake 2.5 miles long, half a mile wide and up to 150 feet deep. It is currently operated by United Utilities as a reservoir and supplies water to West Cumbria. Fortunately, its appearance is barely affected by low and largely unobtrusive engineering works ringing the western end of the lake.

Although swimming is not permitted you are allowed to put a canoe or boat on the water without power or sail. Groups do require a permit and I suggest you contact United Utilities, care of the Thirlmere Treatment Works (01768-772334) for further clarification and advice.

Locked gates bar access beyond Bleach Green Car Park (OS Grid Ref: NY085154) and I am forced to wheel the canoe on trolley the final 400 metres to water's edge. The "portage" is not without its problems as I accidentally drop the boat onto my shins en route. Ouch! "Bloodied and bruised" I may be, but at least a quick inspection reveals no obvious damage done to the boat!

Although much of the western shore is fenced off I discover a convenient strip of shingle beach shielded by a low green protective moraine, to the immediate southern end of the outfall weir, to launch my boat (OS Grid Ref: NY089151).

I am finally afloat for 12:35pm. And it is an absolute joy to be rowing on waters so still, so tranquil and so crystal clear. The lower lake is wide and fringed by a patchwork of fields and sweep of rolling hills. It really is picturesque.

And I am delighted to encounter Roger, a fellow paddler from the nearby town of Workington, on the water. "The first time you've rowed here?" he repeats incredulously whilst skilfully manoeuvring his bright yellow canoe to remain within speaking distance. He is returning to Bowness Knott Car Park after completing an early morning tour of the lake.

It is evidently one of his favourite and most paddled lakes. He recounts that he and his partner once drove over to Thirlmere "for a change of scenery" but they were so dismayed by the state of the Armboth launch site that they didn't even bother putting boats to water. We finally wish each other well and continue our separate journeys.

Surprising it may be, but this lake has had its "celebrity moments", none more so than the time that it was visited by the former US president Bill Clinton and first Lady, Hillary (nee Rodham) in the spring of 1973!

Both have written in their separate memoirs that Bill proposed "at twilight" on the shores of Ennerdale Water. Magical the setting may have been but Hillary, allegedly, refused to say "yes" there and then but made him wait a further two years until she finally agreed to marry him in his home state of Arkansas!

The upper lake narrows as it squeezes between steep plunging flanks. The early afternoon sun lingers low over the southern horizon as I round close under Angler's Crag, a towering rocky promontory drenched in sombre shade. Beyond, the lower slopes are bristling with acres upon acres of regimented coniferous forest, their lines marching regardless of fractured terrain.

I'm fascinated by that group of black cormorants and dull grey gulls making precarious perch on the so-called "Little Isle"; this small rocky prominence barely breaks the surface mid lake between Angler's Crag and Bowness Knott.

Inviolate the lake may appear but its sanctity has been bitterly contested. Both British Nuclear Fuels Limited (BNFL) and North West Water Authority (NWWA) applied in the 1970s to draw additional water from the lake. Their proposals would have resulted in the construction of a huge impounding embankment together with a horrible "tidal" scar encircling what was left of the original lake shore.

A Public Enquiry was held and, fortunately for all lovers of the Lake District, the then Secretary of State, Michael Heseltine, rejected both proposals for a variety of reasons.

Waves strengthen as I reach the far, eastern indented shore (OS Grid Ref: NY125142) and I struggle to turn round and head back for "home". There is a beguiling beauty and solemnity about the upper valley that inspires me to want to explore further. Savage peaks overlap further than the eye can imagine, and so it is no real surprise to learn that this valley should also play host to the loneliest youth hostel in the Lake District at Black Sail.

Slap…slap…slap…! Oncoming waves, driven by a rising westerly, crash repeatedly into the flattened bow on my laboured return with annoying regularity. Occasionally, a rogue wave breaks over the bow and water pours into the boat, most unpleasantly.

No wonder I rush over to shelter in the windless lee of Bowness Knott! "Plain sailing" resumes once I regain the lower lake and aim for my original launch spot. I am relieved to make an unhurried and gentle, trouble free landing for 2:45pm.

Barely have I time to drag the boat up the shingle beach out of harm's way than I am suddenly confronted by a most unpleasant local angler who rushes over to accuse me of fishing illegally on "his lake". This proves a most unfortunate "blot" on the afternoon and I send him away with a flea in his ear.

He is the exception. I am impressed by everyone else's interest in my project and obvious affection for what they deem "their" lake; none more so than that kind couple who take time to tell me about the ground breaking "Wild Ennerdale Project".

This was founded in 2002 as a partnership of people and organisations and has an inspiring vision "…to allow the evolution of Ennerdale as a wild valley for the benefit of people, relying more on natural processes to

shape its landscape and ecology….". It is led by the three principal land owners in the valley, namely United Utilities, National Trust and Forestry Commission, with the support of Natural England.

Ennerdale is home to England's only migrating population of the rare and endangered arctic char. And it is heartening

82

to learn that the Project has already managed to bring this rare and endangered fish back from what was almost the brink of extinction.

Resembling the trout in size and appearance and dating back to the Ice Age, the arctic char is particularly sensitive to acidic waters. The Project has helped create more favourable conditions for its survival by reducing barriers to migration, improving conditions for nesting and felling 150 hectares of those "acidic" coniferous plantations. Recent surveys have already shown there to have been a marked increase in the numbers of char in Ennerdale since the project began.

And there is even more good news; the Environment Agency recently announced that it intends to withdraw its abstraction licence from Ennerdale Water in 2025. This is bound to create significant changes to the lake and also, hopefully, present new opportunities for all its users.

NB Canoeists are asked not to paddle in the upper 3km of the River Ehen immediately downstream of Ennerdale Water as it supports a large and rare population of freshwater pearl mussels.

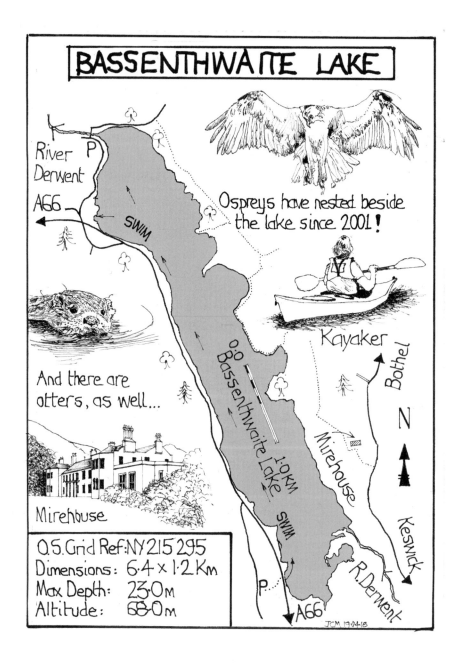

BASSENTHWAITE LAKE

Ospreys have nested beside the lake since 2001!

River Derwent
A66

P

SWIM

And there are otters, as well...

Mirehouse

0.0
Bassenthwaite Lake
1.0 KM

SWIM

Kayaker

Bothel

N

Mirehouse

Keswick

R. Derwent

P

A66

JCM 1994-18

O.S. Grid Ref: NY 215 295
Dimensions: 6.4 × 1.2 Km
Max Depth: 23.0 m
Altitude: 68.0 m

BASSENTHWAITE LAKE (12/17)

Sunday 18 October 2015

Bassenthwaite Lake is Tom and Emma's favourite stretch of water in the Lake District. They love to spend time in the summer swimming in its sheltered eastern bays and picnicking with their young family on its remote shorelines.

Naturally, I am pleased that Tom joins me to swim the length of lake. Despite plummeting temperatures and overnight frosts we reckon that there is still just time for one last outing of the wet suits. Nevertheless, this swim proves a salutary lesson on the perils of outdoor swimming as we underestimate the length of the lake and also misjudge the final part of our route.

Bassenthwaite Lake is the most northerly of the 17 "big lakes" and sits in the remote moorland fringes of the Lake District. Connected to Derwent Water by a short length of the River Derwent, it is 4 miles long, 0.75 miles wide and extremely shallow, being never more than 75 feet deep.

Bassenthwaite Lake possesses a solitary and retiring disposition. It also has its idiosyncrasies. As well as being the only body of water in the Lake District to use the word "lake" in its name – all the others being "waters", "meres" or "tarns" – there is a surprising shift in lake levels. Locals may refer, sarcastically, to this little known phenomenon as the "Bassenthwaite tide" but it should not be underestimated as variations of up to nine feet in lake level have been recorded!

Although much of the lake shore is privately owned, it is possible to swim the entire length of the lake by accessing the two stretches of public shore which are conveniently located at either ends of the western shore. There is only very limited access to parts of the eastern shore.

We plan to swim from south to north, taking advantage of any north bound current within the lake. We drive to Powter Howe Car Park (OS Grid Ref: NY220265), located near the southern end of the lake a little before noon. The place is near deserted as we change into our wet suits and follow a half mile path clambering round the base of Powter Howe Wood before dropping down to lake shore (OS Grid Ref: NY223268).

Conditions appear near perfect. The glassy mirrored surface of the lake is as still as a proverbial mill pond. Although there isn't the slightest hint of a breeze to spoil proceedings, our initial dip of the toes into the shallow waters of the near western bay reveals that it is a very cold 11 degrees Centigrade! Fortunately, there is no one to watch our laboured pantomimings as we slip and stumble over large and rounded pebbles.

Eventually we reach deeper waters and begin to swim. I know that you are supposed to take the first mile steadily, but we quickly break into strong powerful racing breaststrokes in the hope that the effort will help warm up our desperately cold feet and hands.

Of course safety is always paramount and I strap an orange tow float to my waist for visibility's sake. We are lucky to have the lake to ourselves, as foolishly, I have left it too late to arrange any boat cover. I had previously left a message with Bassenthwaite Sailing Club (017687-76341) to warn them of our passage but their planned open event is cancelled due to"…a complete absence of wind….".

It is a privilege to swim in these conditions. The lake is vast, wide and still. The glassy surface is disturbed only by our hurried motion, as a myriad of ripples from our determined wake extend an eternity. The feeling is quite extraordinary. And views across the lake towards Skiddaw's gaunt slate flanks are impressive. They tower high over purple fells and green afforested hills tumbling down to the eastern shoreline.

We swim beside a dramatic western shoreline, ablaze with broad leafed woodland. Autumn provides an intoxicating display of leaves coloured a variety of golden brown, tinged with glints of red and burnished yellow. It takes half an hour to warm up and get into our stroke. This may be Tom's only long swim of the season, but he soon powers ahead only pausing briefly to switch between crawl and breaststroke. And to think that he has only just returned to Cumbria after undertaking an arduous fortnight of caving in Northern Spain....

We soon settle into a routine. We quickly learn to ignore the constant rumble of traffic making indecent haste on the adjoining A66 and head out into the lake to avoid a group of anglers scattered about a wooded bay. It is reassuring to realise that a powerful current is pushing us forever northwards.

The lake plays host to an impressive array of wintering wild fowl and wide variety of fish. Although Atlantic salmon and the elusive sea lamprey come to spawn in the lake and its tributaries, recent evidence suggests that a colony of rare vendace, a native freshwater fish, also inhabits the lake.

No matter, few could have dared hope, in their wildest dreams, that a pair of breeding ospreys would settle on the lake in 2001. It is sobering to realise that breeding ospreys had been extinct in England since 1842, and we are extremely lucky that pairs of birds have been returning each spring from their annual winter migration to Africa to raise over 20 chicks in

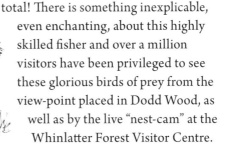

total! There is something inexplicable, even enchanting, about this highly skilled fisher and over a million visitors have been privileged to see these glorious birds of prey from the view-point placed in Dodd Wood, as well as by the live "nest-cam" at the Whinlatter Forest Visitor Centre.

One mile gone and we continue to pursue a brisk punishing pace. I realise that I've strayed far too far from shore and alter my line to stay "within earshot" of Tom. He suggests that we aim for "the distant headland". It does seem a long way off and I worry that the opaque water really chills every time that I try and immerse my face to extend the glide in my racing breaststroke.

Our progress appears imperceptible, lost in the vastness of nature's silence. The scenery changes subtly as we advance down the lake. Long gone is Skiddaw's crowning mantle for a land of bucolic and rolling gentle hills. Historic houses and yeoman farmsteads cling to perilous slopes. Lonely St

Bega's church is said to have been sited deliberately in such a remote bay of the eastern shore "to avoid marauders". The wide sweep of Scarness Bay protects a delightful boat house.

Splendid the lake may appear but the Lake District National Park Authority was so concerned by a drastic deterioration in the quality of the lake's water in recent years that it was forced to declare that the lake was "in the balance" and initiated the "Still Waters, Bassenthwaite Lake Restoration Programme" to improve matters.

Subsequently, the Bassenthwaite Reflections was formed between 2008 and 2010. This community focused Landscape Partnership Scheme contributed to the preservation, restoration and protection of the area's ecology and natural habitats; encouraged the community to develop an appreciation and understanding of the value of the landscape and wildlife; and to take a more active role in looking after it.

In addition, United Utilities upgraded their waste water treatment works to reduce the amount of phosphate pollution entering the lake and the Forestry Commission improved tree cover to lessen soil erosion. But the threat from invasive fish and plant species remains.

There is an impermanence and vitality about any large stretch of water that can both attract and also terrify, and I must admit to suffering occasionally in the final thirty minutes of the swim it takes to reach that wooded headland. And it's a fearsomely steep and inhospitable God-forsaken looking spot to boot. I welcome a sudden "grounding" on a hidden sand bank to give me the opportunity to briefly rest my aching thighs and calves!

The shoreline changes beyond Peel Wyke Bridge and public boat launch site. Unfortunately, we now make a "navigational error" as we round the headland rather than striking out "due north" across the lake towards our rightful destination at Banks Point (OS Grid Ref: NY202317).

We chase an indistinct shoreline, lost within extensive acres of reed beds, little realising that we have strayed into a side channel. Soon we find ourselves sprawling in shallow waters and grounded in a weave of infinite New Zealand pigmyweed. Talk about being stranded up a side creek without a proverbial paddle!

We have come far enough, having swum an estimated 3.75 miles, and, quite honestly, neither of us has the appetite to "double back" and commit to crossing the final bay in front of the Bassenthwaite Sailing Club. It is just too risky without boat support.

We leave the lake just short of our final finishing point and resort to "shanks's ponies" for the last quarter mile to reach Tom's car at Banks Point Car Park (OS Grid Ref: NY201320). This has been quite an extraordinary adventure and serves as a fitting conclusion to what has been yet another successful season of swimming!

PS The Lake District National Park Authority owns the lake and only allows craft to access the lake from the launch site at Peel Wyke. Users also have to obtain a permit for their crafts from the LDNPA.

A MOST EXTRAORDINARY JOURNEY

Open Water Swimming is definitely "flavour of the month". And it now seems that barely a month seems to go by without news breaking of wet suited adventurers completing maiden swims down the length of rivers, be it the River Eden in Cumbria or even the River Severn, the longest river in the United Kingdom.

But, surely Sean Conway "takes the biscuit" for being the first person to swim the length of Great Britain? I listen spellbound as he recounts his exploits to a captivated audience at the Kendal Mountain Festival in November 2015. The talk is both inspiring and incredible.

Sean Conway is recognisable for his unkempt red hair and bushy beard. Of course appearances can be deceptive; after all he cycled around the world in 2012 and recently became the first person to complete the "ultimate triathlon", swimming, cycling and running the length of the country. It wasn't always thus. He recounts giving up a miserable and unfulfilling existence as a corporate photographer in London for a life of adventure and challenge in 2011.

Sean readily admits that this swim was a tough challenge! He recounts how he overcame so many challenges even starting his venture, thanks to a lack of funds and so many people telling him "it can't be done". And it took him twice as long to complete as he first imagined.

The statistics speak for themselves. He took 135 days to swim from Land's End to John O'Groats, wearing out three wet suits and losing 10% of his body weight in the process. Ninety of the days were spent swimming whilst the remaining forty five days were lost on account of bad weather, contrary tides and rest.

I can't help but think that some of the issues are self-imposed. Incredible though it may seem, he admits to never having swum in the sea before setting out from Land's End on 30th June 2013. No wonder that both he and his three man volunteer crew manning his support yacht were all sea sick within an hour of "casting off"!

Arrangements may appear chaotic but the expedition soon settles into a glorious sounding routine. Idyllic days are spent swimming along the

Cornish coast and nights are spent barbecuing freshly caught fish in remote Cornish coves.

Sean insists that you must run the project, rather than letting the project run you. It is a fair point. Even so, I struggle to understand why they decide to head over to Ireland "for the hell of it" because none of them had been there before!

Nevertheless, it proved an inspired decision. Despite a "scary" crossing of a 20mile wide shipping lane and shoals of nasty stinging lion maned jelly fish, he was blessed with wonderfully flat calm seas along Ireland's sheltered eastern coast. And there were moments of sheer magic, complete with night time swimming in the phosphorescent waters of the Irish Sea and also encountering seals and dolphins.

He readily admits to underestimating the enormity of the swim in Scotland and it is evident that the swim up the indented west coast of Scotland had its moments, not least crossing the formidable Gulf of Correyvreckan, threatening the unwary in the straits separating the islands of Jura and Harris.

He says that the fear of failure spurs him on and he admits that at times he doubted whether he would ever complete the project, fully aware that the nights were closing in and water temperatures were tumbling with the arrival of winter. But I wonder. Surely he is addicted to taking risk; the greater and more extreme the risk the better, it would seem.

Sure enough, near disaster looms when the expedition attempts to round the notorious Cape Wrath, in a Force 8 winter gale. Conditions were bad enough to slip the anchor from the yacht, flip over the semi rigid inflatable and smash the kayak in two!

They do say that the brave make their own luck. And he was extremely fortunate to enjoy a three day break in the weather to complete the final section of the swim and finish in John o'Groats on 11 November 2013!

"I even made the inside pages of "The Times"" he chuckles delightedly on recounting being met by the world's media and a well-meaning crowd of champagne popping friends and well wishers.

And spare a thought for his companion, Emily Bell, who followed alongside his every stroke in a kayak, despite her fear of open water, and unintentionally became the first person to canoe the entire length of Great Britain in the bargain!

How can I not fail to be impressed by his achievements and final pronouncement that: "You must always aim higher". It is good advice. His message inspires me to press on, despite some extremely challenging circumstances in the year ahead.

YEAR THREE
CHALLENGING SWIMS

It is hard to appreciate the amount of flooding, the extent of devastation or the cost of human misery imposed by Storm Desmond on the County of Cumbria, and the Lake District in particular, on the 5th December 2015.

At times, you wondered if the region could ever recover. But it has. And that is due in no small part to the locals; it is as well that they are made of stern stiff. Time marches on and the County is keen to show that it is still open for business.

I also realise that I need to prepare for an extremely busy and testing summer of truly challenging swims including both Ullswater and Windermere "end to end". And so, I sign up for the "Epic Events" organised mass swim of Derwent Water scheduled for early June as a training session. The sun is exceptionally strong and the water is unbelievably warm and flat calm. It is an absolute joy to experience the town crowded, the lake busy and everyone enjoying themselves. What a contrast from 6 months ago when so much damage was caused to the town and lake.

I arrive early at Keswick to help set up the race at lake side; it is an opportunity to reacquaint myself with fellow marshals, and also bump into Carlisle swimmers, Richard and Janet, yet again, as they just happen to be taking a very early morning dip in the lake!

"Epic Events" have scheduled 3 swims of 500m, 1 mile and 3.8km duration. I enter the 3.8km distance swim, the second event of the day.

This entails swimming three circuits of a roughly oblong shaped course encircling the wooded Derwent Isle.

Even though I am none too keen to overtax myself so early in the season, I believe that this swim is one of the most enjoyable swims I have ever encountered for reasons of favourable conditions and achievement. Swimmers set off at a fierce pace and I follow in their slip stream as we head for the first of many inflatable yellow marker buoys.

After shaking off two freestylers at the end of the first circuit, I swim on my own for much of the remaining course and rely on overtaking racers and safety canoes for steering in the right direction. The swim is pure bliss, and I still have enough head of steam left to hunt down a tiring freestyler on the final run! I finish in a very respectable time of 1 hour 52 minutes 8.9 seconds.

But spare a thought for Jordan, one of our lake swimmers, who comes first in the one mile event in a strong time of 19 minutes 21.85 seconds. How, indeed, do you beat that!

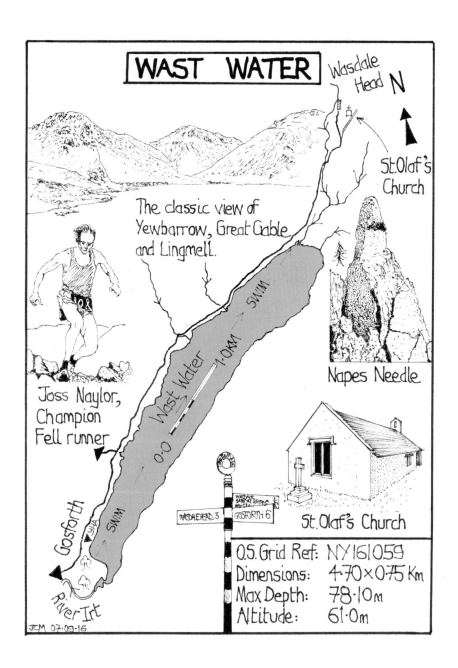

WAST WATER

Wasdale Head N

St.Olaf's Church

The classic view of Yewbarrow, Great Gable and Lingmell.

SWIM

1.0 KM

Wast Water

0.0

SWIM

Napes Needle

Joss Naylor, Champion Fell runner

Gosforth

SWIM

River Irt

WASDALE HEAD 3

GOSFORTH 6

St.Olaf's Church

O.S. Grid Ref:	NY161059
Dimensions:	4·70 × 0·75 Km
Max Depth:	78·10m
Altitude:	61·0m

JCM 07·09·16

WAST WATER (13/17)

Tuesday 12 July 2016

Swimming in Wast Water is both challenging and exhilarating at the best of times. There is an elemental savagery about the inspirational setting and mountain scenery that literally takes your breath away.

Although Wast Water is not a particularly large stretch of water by Lake District standards, being a mere 3 miles long by 0.5 miles wide, its waters have a fearsome reputation for being the coldest and the deepest of the lakes.

So cold, in fact, that I have even been advised to delay my swim until later in the season when its frigid waters should have warmed up a smidgen. Unfortunately, I don't have the luxury of time as I intend to use this swim as a dress rehearsal for a lengthy swim in Ullswater scheduled for later in the month. I am fortunate that Andy is keen to accompany me with his inflatable canoe.

Wast Water occupies the greater part of the remote Wasdale valley. This is situated in the south west of the county and is not an easy place to access. A difficult road twists and turns the length of the valley all the way to the isolated Wasdale Head with its scatter of inn, tiny church and farm buildings, for good measure.

Conditions are near perfect for swimming; the afternoon sun shines gloriously and the water is an unbelievably flat calm. But there is no room for complacency and it is vital that we thoroughly "recce" the lake and agree suitable start and finish points before commencing.

Andy recommends swimming the length of the lake from west to east, i.e. from Santon to Wasdale Head. This is against the current but takes advantage of any prevailing westerly wind. And if I'm not going to enjoy swimming towards those charismatic mountains dominating the head of the valley, then what on earth will I enjoy?

We drive back down the valley and park at the roadside (OS Grid Ref NY148049) and unload our kit. Whilst Andy prepares to inflate and launch the canoe, I don the wetsuit and follow the permitted path along the north shore to lake-end (OS Grid Ref NY145043).

A fine shingle beach leads quickly into knee deep water. I kick off tentatively and take a while to get into my stride. Even though the water doesn't feel anywhere near as lung gasping cold as I first feared, I still suffer a sore and painfully throbbing headache as soon as I dip my head under water and test out a few, full blooded racing strokes. This condition is known in swimming circles as an "ice cream head" for obvious reasons....

Andy is paddling energetically down the lake and soon meets me. It soon becomes abundantly clear that we have the entire lake to ourselves! And Andy's inspired decision that we should head "straight down the centre" of the lake only adds to the splendour of our adventure. It is bizarre; all I need do is aim for the peak of Great Gable and race away. That mile long section of plunging screes dominating the southern shore appears even more impressive when viewed from the water rather than roadside.

It is galling to recount that I first set eyes on this exhilarating valley way back in 1973 when scrambling the "Climber's Traverse" of Great Gable and successfully "threading Napes Needle", probably the most famous piece of rock in the country. Hackneyed it may sound but I knew, then and there, that I wanted to spend the rest of my life in Cumbria....

Superlatives abound about every aspect of this special valley. So it is not really so surprising to discover that the valley is also known as the birthplace of British Mountaineering, and that the Wasdale Head Hotel became the base for aspiring Victorian mountaineers.

I sense a slight twinge of cramp in my right calf as I halt at mid lake (1.5miles) to gulp down an energy gel. The westerly wind freshens and waves break awkwardly as I encounter the outfall of Nether Beck; I must

put down my head and push on regardless. Two miles completed and I feel both my hamstrings beginning to tighten, most uncharacteristically.

I cannot fail to mention Joss Naylor MBE, the celebrated fell runner and much respected fell farmer, who hails from this valley. Although he is now in his eighties, it does not seem so long ago that "The Incredible Joss", as he is still known in these parts, made the national headlines for his ability to run 72 Lakeland peaks in under 24 hours with time to spare. His record has lasted over forty years.

Andy forges desperately ahead as we approach our "finishing line" at the top of the lake. It is always a marvellous feeling to be nearing the end of any long swim and I am especially pleased to be completing this journey as it has proved to be both physically and mentally demanding. We purposefully chose our landing spot to be conveniently close to the adjoining roadside (OS Grid Ref: NY178074).

I totter the last few vital metres of lake before collapsing, with relief, on the grass lined shoreline. Now I can finally peel out of the wet suit! Sadly there is hardly any rest for "the wicked" as we both need to retrieve our spare clothes and outstanding kit previously deposited on the road side.

It may not be far away but this is easier said than done as we are separated from the road by a steep slope which is covered in near impenetrable and shoulder high bracken. Desperate is our attempt at beating a path using Andy's paddle and progress is hindered by nasty strands of brambles that snag, jag and tear our bare legs and feet something horrible.

Eventually we emerge at roadside, bloodied but victorious. How fortune that Andy had the presence of mind to leave a bicycle at roadside on which he proceeds to cycle down the valley to collect the car.

NB. The National Trust owns the lake and most of the surrounding land and only allows a maximum of 15 canoes and rowing boats on the water at any one time; power boats and sail craft are not permitted.

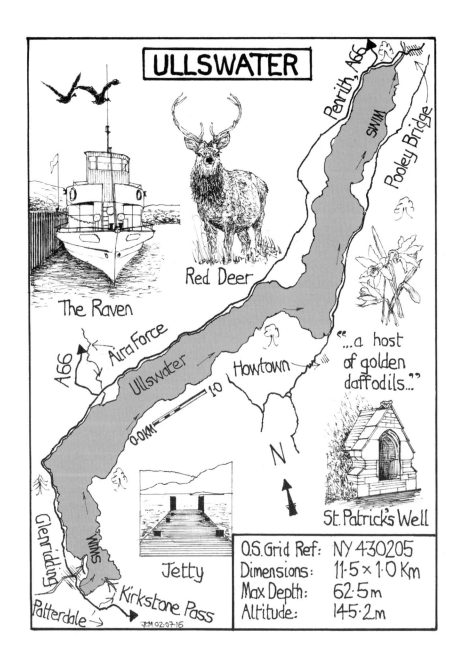

ULLSWATER

Penrith, A66

SWIM

Pooley Bridge

Red Deer

The Raven

A66

Aira Force

Ullswater

Howtown

SWIM

"...a host of golden daffodils..."

1·0

0·0 KM

N

St. Patrick's Well

Jetty

Glenridding

SWIM

Patterdale →

Kirkstone Pass

JCM 02·07·16

O.S. Grid Ref:	NY 430205
Dimensions:	11·5 × 1·0 Km
Max Depth:	62·5 m
Altitude:	145·2 m

ULLSWATER (14/17)

Saturday 30 July 2016

Ullswater is a splendid lake and rightly called "The Queen of the Lakes". At 7.5 miles in length, it is not only the second largest but also widely known as the second coldest of all the lakes.

Many regard Ullswater as more of an inland sea than a mere lake, such is its reputation for harbouring capricious winds and contrary currents that present a serious challenge to any sailor, never mind long distance swimmer. I am under no illusion as to the challenge involved in swimming the lake in one go.

I am conscious that the lake and surroundings suffered more than their fair share from the effects of Storm Desmond that devastated so much of Cumbria in December 2015. As well as causing the collapse of the historic bridge at Pooley Bridge, Glenridding was flooded any number of times.

The storm even caused flooding to Wigton Baths, a community run swimming pool near my home in north western Cumbria. Although Cumbrians are, by nature, hardy and resilient some people's desperate plight made me wonder if I could help in any way. And so I came up with an idea of promoting my Ullswater swim as a means of celebrating the recovery of the Lake District and also taking the opportunity to raise much needed cash for Wigton Baths Trust.

My project seems to have caught the public imagination and I am featured in several local newspapers and publications in the weeks building up to the swim. I am even interviewed live on BBC Cumbria Local Radio "breakfast show" on the shores of the lake at Pooley Bridge on the morning of the swim.

"And what's the weather like?" wonders the popular presenter, Mike Zeller.

"I think I'm blessed, "I respond, "It appears dead calm, there's a light westerly breeze and it's gloriously dry!" The interview goes well and we continue chatting; he wants to know all about my swimming exploits and adventures. Game on! And now for the easy bit: swimming....

We meet up at St. Patrick's Boat Landing (017684-82393), Patterdale, (OS Grid Ref: NY388166) located on the south western shore of the lake. It is fitting that I am joined by Sam, a lifeguard at Wigton Baths and experienced triathlete who is going to swim a couple of miles with me. We are supported by my niece and nephew, Laura and Robbie, who will be crewing a hired fishing boat along with Caroline and sea kayak. Caroline's knowledge of the lake and advice proves absolutely fundamental to the success of the day. (Fishing boats are only available for swimming outside the fishing season.)

So many plates to keep spinning! Organising a sponsored swim in a crowded lake is no simple undertaking and I hate to think of the number of e-mails I send and phone calls I make to advertise the swim, never mind ensure that those organisations affected by my lake are informed of my swim route and timings. It is imperative that both the LDNPA Lake Ranger Team (0844-2252922) and the Ullswater Steamship Company (017684 82229) are fully aware of my project.

10:00am. Cheers, generous applause and heartfelt cries of "Good Luck" from the assembled throng of well-wishers and Wigton Baths' supporters echo the bay as Sam and I step into the water and set off swimming.

Caroline struggles to keep up with Sam as she immediately powers off in a frenzy of freestyle, all whirring arms and legs, on her two mile swim. She puts my leisurely pace to shame! Robbie grabs the oars in the fishing boat and he begins to row alongside me whilst Laura navigates assiduously.

Ullswater is unique in the Lake District as it is formed with three distinct alignments, or reaches, that cleave their way through the most dramatic of surrounding mountains and hills. And attempting to swim the shortest length of such a crooked lake is not easy.

Gerrard Smith, the boat yard owner, recommends that I should swim the lake from south to north "as most swimmers take advantage of a strong lake current". And so I plan to follow the eastern shore for the first half of the lake, before crossing the lake at mid-point near Howtown Bay and continuing the upper half alongside the western shore all the way to Pooley Bridge.

This is by far the longest swim I have ever undertaken. I desperately realise the need to conserve energy so I resolve to slow down my usual racing stroke, prolonging the glide and extending the short break between arm pull and leg kick.

Purposefully avoiding the nearby "Spit" with Ullswater Steamer in jetty, we strike across the lower reach and follow the eastern coastline, encircling the base of mighty Place Fell. It proves a dramatic and indented shore line. Rocks brush under me as we steer close under the Devil's Chimney cliff.

The water is green and opaque and reasonably warm. Perhaps we are lulled into false security by the sheltered, calm waters of the southern reach? I celebrate completing my first mile by gulping down most of the contents of a rogue wave whilst chatting to Robbie and Laura! Thank goodness this wasn't salt water or I might well be in real trouble as trapped salt water in the lungs tends to draw in yet more water!

My swim is well advertised and passengers wave enthusiastically from crowded decks fore and aft as the first of many an evocative glistening white liveried Ullswater Steamer passes by. Sustained surges of breaking waves follow in their wakes as they ply their busy trade twixt Glenridding, Howtown and Pooley Bridge. Of course, we've hoisted our blue and white alpha flag, even though it is widely rumoured that not all the "weekend" sailors really know, or care, what it signifies....

Caroline returns to announce that Sam has already completed her two mile swim and is now running back on the shore path to the boat yard in her bare feet as she forgot to pack her flip flops! That is some hardy young woman!

Westerly winds start to strengthen as we gain the middle reach. Ullswater has many historical and literary associations but the best known must be connected with William Wordsworth who was so inspired by a spring walk in Glencoyne Park in 1802 that he later penned those immortal words: "....I wandered lonely as a cloud.......a host of golden daffodils..."

Caroline has an uncanny knack of locating any number of sheltered beaches for feeding spots. And the tiny shingle beach she selects this side of Sandwick Bay could well come out straight out of a "Swallows and Amazons" story line! No matter, Robbie misjudges his footing as he steps off the boat and ends up falling flat into the water, much to everyone else's amusement! He is absolutely soaking.

She insists that I take on water as well as energy giving jelly beans as she fears that I'll become dehydrated from the day's efforts. I appreciate her advice and normal forward motion is soon resumed.

Ullswater is undoubtedly a picturesque lake but the surrounding fells still bear the scars of heavy industry. Glenridding was once regarded as the most important lead mining village in Britain and locals say that the fishing improved considerably after the mines closed in 1962! This has helped nurture the schelly (Coregonus stigmaticus) a freshwater fish of the salmon family, endemic to only four lakes in the Lake District.

In the same year, Lord Birkett of Ulverston saved the lake from further possible environmental damage by an impassioned speech in the House of Lords criticising elements of Manchester Corporation's bill which proposed the impounding of the lake and drawing off additional waters to Haweswater.

4 miles gone. A group of enthusiastic "tombstoners" break off their summit top antics to cheer me on as we round the base of Kailpot Crag and halt

in a rocky inlet tucked away in the corner for a well-earned thirty minute break. It's an opportunity to review our route and have some belated lunch. I partake of a snack of mashed pilchards, half a banana and drink yet more water.

Of course consuming the right sort of food is vital for distance swimming. The web offers all sorts of misleading and contradictory dietary advice and I am indebted to "Science in Sports" (SIS) for recommending a pre swim diet, swim supplements and after swim rapid recovery drink. Their emphasis on the importance of carbohydrates in the vital 36 hours pre swim led me to consume significant quantities of porridge, bananas, bread, pasta and potatoes with all my meals.

Equally, the ability to adapt our plan to prevailing conditions is crucial to both the success and, much more importantly, the safety of our swim. This is plainly all too evident as we approach Howtown Bay and I contemplate my plan to cross the lake in head on waves. Blimey! Conditions are bad enough to swamp the boats, never mind "Muggins"!

Caroline, wisely, recommends that we continue along the eastern shore, following a longer, but far less hazardous route. Nevertheless, we still to have to cross Howtown Bay. Journeying this large stretch of animated water proves some rare adventure! Talk about stepping out of the frying pan and into the fire: no sooner have we reached the "safety" of the far shore than we are buffeted by a fierce squall that is as intense as short lived.

A Rubicon has been passed. We are now entering the third and final reach of the lake. My shoulders begin to ache from the sustained effort and I follow Caroline closely as she squeezes around the heavily wooded and indented shoreline beyond. And Robbie continues to row effortlessly, alongside me.

A gleaming speed boat races across the wide open expanse beyond as we approach the iconic Sharrow Bay Country House Hotel. I suspect that the pilot is edging a shade close to the lake's speed limit of 10mph. This was imposed in July 1983, and I think that he's forgotten that the days of Donald Campbell breaking the world water speed record of 202mph on this lake in 1955 have long been consigned to the history books.....

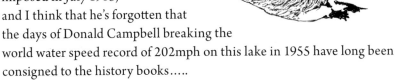

A significant change in the scenery is apparent as we progress the third reach; gone are steep mountains for low, rolling uplands as pastoral interludes lap down to water's edge.

On rounding Thwaitehill Neb, we can finally see the end of the lake! Now I feel confident enough to believe that I can complete the task!! Yes, it has taken much longer than I originally envisaged but what the heck? It proves a lovely sunny evening and, quite honestly, what else would I want to be doing?

6.5 miles: Lines of gleaming yachts extend a near eternity as we pass Ullswater Sailing Club. So near, so far. And that is the inevitable dilemma of long distance swimming. Now I am starting to understand what my ex-Channel swimming friends from Dover meant when they described swimming as 10% physical and 90% mental!...Blimey! The final mile takes its toll. I focus on Dunmallard's wooded pike rising above Pooley Bridge and try and ignore the excruciating pain in my right knee every time I execute a leg kick.

The upper bay is shallow and sandy and the near shore is littered with all manner of obstacles ready to snag the unsuspecting swimmer; I've long lost count of the number of times I've collided with submerged boulders and been becalmed by areas of dense, underwater weeds.

Breaking waves from a brisk westerly add a certain drama to the setting as we finally approach Pooley Bridge. I've long been swimming "on empty" and we are joined on the final furlong by a canoeist and swimmer who I am pleased to hear is also an enthusiastic "Epic Events" competitor.

A crowd of assembled Wigton Baths Trust Board members, family and interested on-lookers cheer and clap as I arrive at lake-end and land on the shingle beach on the north eastern lake shore opposite the steamer jetty (O.S. Grid Ref: NY468242).

Emerging from the water like a "Selkie", the mythical sea creature that is supposed to be half man and half seal, I find myself oddly uncertain of my surroundings. My legs and balance have gone and I try and stand up more than once before flopping back into the water. It takes time to adjust.

It is now 7:15pm and I need to consume some rapid recovery drink, strip off the wetsuit and obtain some food. And we still have to get the boats back to the Patterdale Boat Yard.

I am delighted by everyone's generosity as my swim eventually raises over £1,000 for the Wigton Baths Trust.

NB The River Eamont is owned by the Dalemain Estate, and is normally too shallow to swim or canoe.

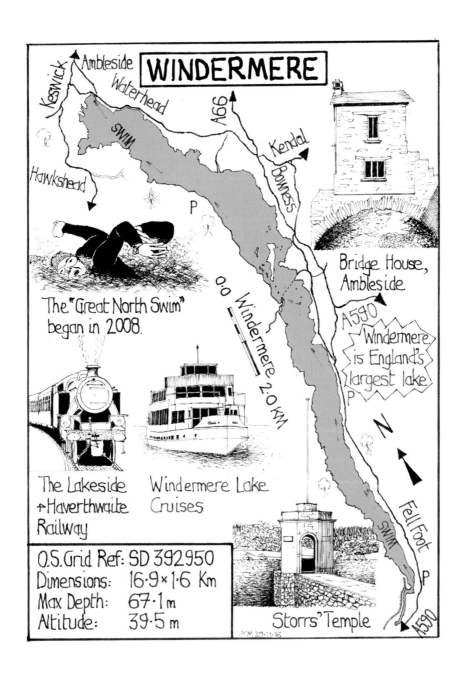

WINDERMERE

Keswick

Ambleside

Waterhead

A66

Kendal

SWIM

Bowness

Hawkshead

P

Bridge House, Ambleside

The "Great North Swim" began in 2008.

0·0 Windermere 2·0 KM

A590

Windermere is England's largest lake

P

N

The Lakeside + Haverthwaite Railway

Windermere Lake Cruises

SWIM

Fell Foot

P

Storrs' Temple

A590

O.S. Grid Ref:	SD 392 950
Dimensions:	16·9 × 1·6 Km
Max Depth:	67·1 m
Altitude:	39·5 m

JCM 29·11·16

WINDERMERE (15/17)

Friday 9 to Sunday 11 September 2016

It has to be said that swimming the 10.5 miles length of Windermere, England's longest and busiest lake, isn't going to be easy; in fact the sheer size of the lake literally takes your breath away.

Windermere easily dwarfs Ullswater, the second largest lake in the Lake District. And if that can be likened to a sea, then Windermere must be regarded, and, more importantly, respected as an ocean. So testing is the challenge that many "end to end" swimmers treat the hard earned experience as a dress rehearsal for a subsequent crossing of the English Channel.

I am in illustrious company. In the weeks leading up to my swim I investigate the history of the early lake swimmers. Records are sketchy, at best, but I learn that Captain Webb, the first man to swim the English Channel in 1875, declared on his one and only visit to Windermere Swimming Club that conditions were too trying to attempt a crossing of the lake. And that was despite training for his Channel swim in Lancashire's Hollingworth Lake in near freezing conditions!

I eventually discover that Joseph D. Foster of Oldham Swimming Club appears to be the first man to swim the lake "end to end". He completed this task on Saturday 2nd September 1911 in a time of 11 hours 29 minutes. According to a contemporary newspaper report "…On Friday, he started from Lakeside with the intention of going right through to Ambleside, but owing to the prevalence of a very high wind and rough water he could get no further than Belle Isle, which is about mid way. On Saturday morning, undeterred by this temporary failure, Foster made another attempt, this time starting from Ambleside. Swimming powerfully throughout, he successfully covered the whole distance, about 10.5 miles, and received a hearty welcome from a number of friends and other spectators on the bank…"

Foster led an extraordinary life. After emigrating to Australia in 1914, he served in the Australian and New Zealand Army Corps (ANZACs) in the First World War and was wounded at Gallipoli, Turkey, in 1915. He lived the remainder of his life in Auckland, New Zealand, and continued to take part in long distance swims in New Zealand until well into his 60s.

It says something of Foster's endurance that no one attempted to repeat his swim for another 22 years. The challenge of swimming Windermere "end to end" gained in popularity in the years following the ending of the Second World War and, in 1951, 19 year old Kathleen Mayoh (aka Mrs Kathleen Taylor) of Farnworth, Bolton, was celebrated for becoming the first woman to swim the lake end to end in a time of 10 hours 2 minutes.

Unfortunately, my initial attempts to swim in an organised event prove futile. Whilst I would dearly love to take part in the British Long Distance Swimming Association's (BLDSA) annual end to end lake championships in September, I realise that I am neither fit, nor hardy, enough to swim the lake "bare backed" and in under the requisite eight hour threshold. Strict rules are enforced, and wet suits are not allowed.

Windermere has certainly benefited in recent years from the phenomenal growth of open water swimming and, in particular, the popularity of the annually held "Great North Swim". Lakeside businesses are now offering all sorts of swimming related activities, be they introductory swimming courses, the selling of wet suits and even the organising of "end to end" packages.

I quickly discover that most "end to end" mass swims for wet-suited swimmers are booked up months, if not years, in advance; and I'm put off by the prices that some companies advertise for providing "one to one" support and guidance packages.

Time is pressing so I feel that I have no other option than organising the swim myself if I want to do it this season. Even so, I feel that I really

110

haven't the heart to attempt to swim the entire lake in one go and I plan to complete the swim over three manageable stages in one long weekend.

Obviously there are inherent risks and pitfalls in this approach, and the least said about my initial struggles to book support boat and crews, the better!

Route planning is equally fraught and I am indebted to Thomas G. Noblett, a well-known swimmer and noted Lakeland hotelier, for advising me to: "Head south to north, from Fell Foot to Ambleside. The other way contains far too many false horizons and bays." He should know having swum the lake many times and once even making the "national dailies" for an alleged close encounter with the lake's very own version of Nessie! I have also to thank John McAllister, Carlisle Canoe Club, for supplying me with a very detailed route which he has used when supporting end to end swimmers.

Friday: Fell Foot to Beech Hill

So let's rock and roll! Andy and I begin our preparations for the swim on the shores of the National Trust Fell Foot Park, mid-afternoon, located on the south western tip of the lake (OS Grid Ref: SD381871). It's a lovely spot, proud of its Victorian heritage and splendid parklands which are now definitely showing signs of Autumnal weariness. I have previously checked that we can launch "Palava", Andy's inflatable canoe from their land.

As well as notifying the LDNPA Lake Ranger (0844-2252922), the Windermere Lake Cruises (015394 43360) and the Windermere Ferry of my plan, it is imperative that swimmers phone the South Lakeland District Council Lake Warden (015394 42753) before and after each day's swim for safety's sake. (Not everyone realises that SLDC owns the lake.)

3:30pm. Andy is understandably keen to be off as there is a dreadful weather forecast for this evening and we want to try and miss the worst of it. Fortunately, conditions are predicted to be much more promising for the rest of the weekend.

Anyway, here goes: I take my first tentative step into cold waters and commence a laboured swim against a strong flow of water discharging from the lake southwards into the River Leven!

Windermere consists of two distinct basins occupying the northern and southern halves of the lake. The southern basin is long and narrow and feels enclosed; the northern basin is wide and open. Both basins are separated by a central band of shallows and islets surrounding the wooded mass of Belle Isle.

We plan to follow the plunging and densely wooded eastern shoreline of the southern basin for three or so miles to Beech Hill. Straightaway, I am overwhelmed by the vastness of watery expanse and the sheer silence of afforestation. Familiar mountains are now but mere distant features of a remote Lakeland backcloth, overshadowed by a disturbing vastness of rolling and featureless rises.

Thankfully the passage of those large and gleaming white Windermere Lake Cruisers remind us that we are still actually in the 21st century! They all maintain a respectful distance and speed as they purposefully scarper by...

5:00pm. Progress is steady and we make the 2.5km mark in reasonable spirits, little realising that a rising southerly wind is a portent of imminent rain! The combination of torrential rain and rising wind and waves in the next kilometre makes progress so difficult that we seek the shelter of the windless lee of tree pricked Blake Holme islet for a break. Andy is absolutely soaking and needs to bail out and re-inflate his ailing inflatable canoe before we can continue.

And that is a mere taster of what is to come! Conditions on the final 2.5kms (1.5m) are some of the worst I have ever encountered in open water swimming. The sky darkens prematurely, the wind rises and the rain plummets with an intensity and ferocity that is truly frightening. Despite the night being prematurely "black dark" we must grit our teeth and aim for a barely discernible "headland".

But can we find our landing spot at Beech Hill? I lose sight of Andy more than once as he scurries hither and thither desperate to find some glimmer of shingle beach within the dense undergrowth overhanging the shore.

6:45pm. Eureka! Cold and exhausted we may be but Andy finally lands the canoe and leaps out on to dry land (OS Grid Ref: SD388920)! It is time to strip off the wet suit, don the flip flops and ascend the desperately long and slippery steps leading up the bank to the roadside Car Park. Thank goodness that the toilet facilities are still open and I can change out of the rain. I estimate that I have swum near enough 3.25 miles in 3.25 hours in some atrocious conditions.

Saturday: Beech Hill to Back Barn Jetty

Goodness! What a difference a day makes. I can hardly believe how sunny and warm the day begins; barely a breeze disturbs the calmest of lake waters. It proves ideal for messing about in boats.

Dave B. and Dave C. arrange to meet me at Bowness Bay Marina (015394-45535) and take charge of "Naomi", an electric cabin boat I've hired for the day. And what a real beauty she proves to be! Whilst Isaac, the good natured boat man, delivers a fifteen minute safety briefing to the two Dave's, Muggins prepares to do battle once more with soggy "Speedos" and a still soaking wetsuit. Ugh! (NB. Very few boat companies are prepared to hire out boats to accompany swimmers.)

With the briefing completed, a blue and white alpha flag is strapped securely to the boat, ropes are released and we are away! Mindful that we have to keep at least 30 metres off shore at all times we steer south westwards to Beech Hill. We briefly tie up at the hotel's spindly jetty, just north of last night's landing, where I enter the water at 10:45am (OS Grid Ref SD388921).

Today, I attempt to swim over five miles. This involves completing the length of the southern basin; crossing the line of the Windermere Car Ferry; the central band of islands; and partly heading up the western side of the northern basin. However, even though the water appears nice and warm, I seem to struggle to swim as soon as I start...

11:00am. Barely a quarter of a mile swum and I feel dreadfully out of sorts. Dave B obviously senses that there is something wrong and shouts urgently from the deck: "John! Are you alright?".

I look back at him and mutter something unconvincing.

"You seem to be hardly moving!" he adds in obvious alarm. That frightens me. Last night's swim was not a good experience and it is obvious that it has taken far too much out of me for my own good. Perhaps the enormity of what I am actually trying to achieve is also affecting me because the sudden realisation that I could fail hits me solidly between the eyes. And it hurts, horribly...

It's a cue to shake myself out of my lethargy and try and rally. After all there is still a long, long way to go. Fortunately, I'm nearly restored to full cruising speed by the time that we pass the next indented shoreline and steer towards the Storrs Hotel's jetty, highlighted with a distinctive octagonal tower.

1 mile gone; it is an opportunity to tread water beside the boat and receive a recuperative "Mars Bar" and heartfelt words of encouragement from Dave C: "You're going really well!".

Dave C is particularly concerned about the volume of lake traffic so early in the day and proposes a sensible alternative to my original plan. I had intended to cut diagonally across the middle of the lake to the western shore just south of the landing stage of the cross lake Windermere Car Ferry. Instead, he suggests that we continue heading directly up the eastern shore to Ramp Holme before executing a much shorter and more direct crossing of the lake. It makes good sense.

Somewhere, en route, an inquisitive swan approaches far too close for my liking; elsewhere we steer hard to port to avoid a ring of red warning buoys encircling a hazardous reef.

"Aim for the left hand side of Ramp Holme Island" Dave B advises whilst partaking of yet another cup of steaming coffee from a seemingly endless thermos flask. Certainly, you cannot fail to miss the distinctive island with its steep and heavily afforested sides.

114

I sense the crew's anxiety as we depart the safety of the island and brave the central channel busy with all manner of nautical traffic. Is it any coincidence that the Lake District Warden should speed past in his bright orange semi-rigid inflatable and acknowledge us with a friendly wave as we reach near enough dead centre of the lake?

Reaching the western shore merely signifies the start of our troubles. Now we have to cross over the line of the cable powered car ferry. Timing is crucial and we have to wait for the car ferry to load up its cargo of cars and set off westwards before chancing this vital stretch of water. I respond to the crew's urgency by accelerating the stroke for the few desperate minutes that it takes us to gain calmer waters north of the ferry.

To our left lies Ferry House, the home of the Freshwater Biological Association. As a result of over 75 years research of the lake and its flora and fauna, this charitable body has ensured that the lake is probably one of the best understood in the world. And it certainly teems with life! Besides the predictable pike, perch and trout, the lake supports the prehistoric arctic char, a distant relative of the trout, which has inhabited the lake since the last Ice Age.

And still we have to navigate our way northwards. This involves squeezing "inside" (i.e. to the west) of both Crow and Maiden Holme Islands before bisecting the narrow channel between shore and western base of Belle Isle and then running the gauntlet of the two "Lilies of the Valley" islands. Thank goodness we had the presence of mind to mark Isaac's very clear and detailed instructions on our chart this morning!

Beyond Belle Isle lies the clear and blue open waters of the lake's northern basin. And what a glorious panorama of mountains rises ahead! Such a wonderful afternoon develops as I follow the western shore northwards. Slowly, but surely, the countdown

begins, "Only one mile to go", Dave C suddenly announces and adds with a mischievous chuckle, "It's all downhill from here!".

4:40pm. I finally touch shore on a remote stretch of wooded shore beside the incongruously named and slender Back Barn Jetty reaching far out to water (OS Grid Ref: SD388990). I rest awhile before attempting to stumble, trip and fall over slippery shore-lined boulders. It is time to climb wearily on board "Naomi" and be whisked back to Bowness Bay Marina.

Sunday: Red Nab to Waterhead

A strong southerly blows as I zip up the wet suit one final time early afternoon and await my support boat at the tiny shingle beach beside Red Nab Car Park (OS Grid Ref: SD388994). Is it any wonder that I am now forced to liberally apply lubricating balm over heavily chafed areas at the back of both knees as well as under both arm pits?

Even though I now have only 2.25 miles remaining to complete the swim, I suspect that Lady Windermere has still one or two more mischievous tricks to pull out of that famous handbag to try and thwart my progress...

I am eternally grateful to the Windermere Outdoors Adventure Centre (015394 47183) for offering Josh and his bright orange semi rigid inflatable to escort me on my final segment of the swim; without them, I would have been well and truly scuppered.

We are away for 2:00pm and heading for an hour up the western shore, passing the wooded headland of Watbarrow Point, separating Low and High Wray Bays.

It is hard on days like these to realise that Windermere's water quality has been declining for years and is now affecting several native plants and aquatic species. Competitors in the 2010 Great North Swim are only too aware that the event had to be cancelled as a result of potentially harmful algae bloom which was caused by the excessive amounts of phosphorus in the water.

It is reassuring to know that United Utilities are currently investing in an upgrade of two existing water treatment works and constructing four miles of new sewers in an attempt to restrict the amount of phosphorus entering the lake and hopefully improve water quality.

In addition, the South Cumbria Rivers Trust is taking a new approach to tackling diffuse rural sewage (principally septic tanks) impacting the Windermere catchment.

Josh steers close to my side, to attract my attention and announce, "Over there", whilst pointing in a northerly direction to Waterhead, cowering in the distant bay below towering Fairfield fell. Goodness, it is hard to take in. Can that really be the end of the lake?

"Exposed" is perhaps the best way of describing that final passage of open water; I need to muster all my resolve and something else to take on and survive those surging waves. This surely has to be one of my sternest tests of stamina and resolve in the entire lake challenge.

And all the while Josh races the craft here and there in an effort to draw attention to the many craft of my presence. I rest awhile mid lake to allow the historic Windermere Steam Launch to hurry by; passengers wave and the pilot acknowledges me with a shrill tweet on his steam hooter for good measure!

Curiously, I don't experience the slightest elation as I finally approach Waterhead. Josh carefully guides me past a long line of gleaming yachts anchored off shore before leading me towards the steamer jetty; a ferry is almost ready to be off and we head over to the shore busy with tourists enjoying a lovely day out; few probably care or wonder what I am doing but I need to dig in for the last 100 metres.

I have come far enough (OS Grid Ref: NY378031). It is now 4:20pm and I have swum 2.25 miles in just over 2 hours. There is barely time to celebrate as I am pushed, dragged and hauled somewhat unceremoniously on board prior to a speedy return to Red Nab. And it is a glorious feeling to know that I've successfully completed the swim with only aching shoulders and some chafing to show!

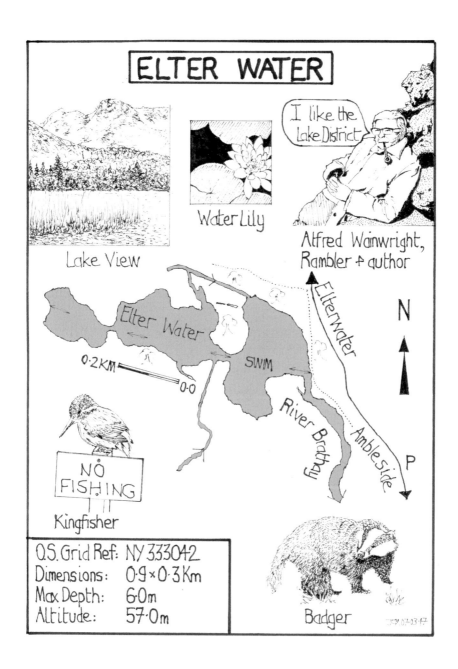

ELTER WATER

Lake View

Water Lily

I like the Lake District

Alfred Wainwright, Rambler & author

Elter Water

Elterwater

SWIM

N

P

0.2 KM

0.0

River Brathay

Ambleside

NO FISHING

Kingfisher

Badger

O.S. Grid Ref: NY 333042
Dimensions: 0.9 × 0.3 Km
Max Depth: 6.0m
Altitude: 57.0m

ELTER WATER (16/17)

Friday 30 September 2016

I am so glad that Tom could join me for my final lake swim in Elter Water as he had accompanied me on our very first foray into Loweswater way back in June 2014.

Not that this was our first attempt at swimming Elter Water. We did intend to swim the lake earlier in the summer but a damning combination of torrential downpours and hold-ups on the M6 motorway south of Carlisle rapidly put paid to that.

It proves well worth the wait, because the day is glorious and this exquisite lake provides a taste of outdoor swimming at its very finest.

We meet up at Silverthwaite Car Park (OS Grid Ref: SD341037) a little before 2:00pm. It is conveniently situated in a disused quarry, a third of a mile from Skelwith Bridge. We change into wet suits and stroll the path alongside the upper River Brathay to gain the south eastern corner of Elter Water (OS Grid Ref: SD339040).

Elter Water is a small lake, barely two thirds of a mile long by a quarter of a mile wide, and consists of three separate but contained pools joined by the narrowest of passageways squeezed between wooded islands. You could be forgiven for thinking that it should be better known as it is strategically located at the junction of the Great and Little Langdale valleys. But it lies largely hidden by dense foliage and is rarely visited.

Although the lake bed is shallow and gently sloping I had not expected the water to feel so cold or appear so fast flowing. What a time for Tom to remind me that it seems even colder than when we last swam together last October in Bassenthwaite Lake. (And neither of us wants to go back there again.....!)

It is not really that surprising; after all, the water flows straight off the fells and is swelled by last night's torrential rain. We swim westwards towards

119

the far side of the first and most easterly of the three pools. Once past the reed beds, we can relax a little and revel in the confined shelter of tranquil waters. Our hands and feet soon begin to warm up.

There is an undeniable serenity about this water that I find absolutely awe inspiring. Even though we are ringed by an extensive circuit of craggy peaks our silent pool is shielded by an impenetrable curtain of reed bed, saplings and dense vegetation.

The narrowest of passageways leads between the southern shore and the wooded mass of Nab Island into the second pool. The gap is shallow and muddy and I crash into more than one half submerged tree trunk; and it hurts!

The water is a haven for wildlife and popular with whooper swans that migrate here in the winter from Scandinavia. Perhaps they've been coming for centuries because the early Viking settlers even named it "swan lake" (elptr vatn) in their honour.

We have to force our way through dense stalks of water lilies littering the second passage to emerge into the third and final pool. Dippers dart fast and low over the water surface as we head for the partially sunken wooden jetty moored in the deserted north western corner of the lake (OS Grid Ref: SD329042). We pause at journey's end to scan the surrounding land; much of which is flat and low lying; an incongruous plantation of spindly Scots pine appears totally out of place...

The Langdales are rightly lauded for their beauty but they have suffered as much as anywhere with a legacy of quarrying and gunpowder manufacture over the centuries; and so it seems quite a privilege to discover this remote corner.

I have to admit that I have started to become" swim-weary" with this summer's efforts and I am more than delighted to finish my swim challenge with such an unexpected revelation. It is time to return and we retrace our outward journey. Now the slight westerly breeze and strong current play to our advantage and we make rapid passage eastwards.

I suppose you could call this final segment our "swan song" as we have to carefully negotiate a family of two adult swans and their four offspring feeding about our starting point. The adult male makes quite a show of his displeasure, complete with aggressive posturing and sustained flapping of wings, but somehow we manage to encircle them carefully and land without any ill effect!

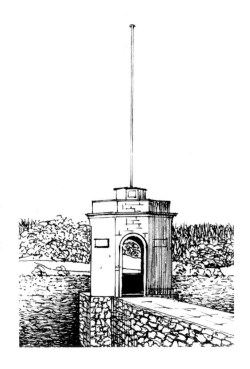

It is now 4:00pm. And I can return to the Silverthwaite Car Park content in the knowledge that my lake challenge is almost complete. Of course, I have still to walk around Esthwaite Water, to say that I have visited every lake, but that can come later....

ESTHWAITE WATER

Coniston

Hawkshead

N

Herdwick Tup

Beatrix Potter at Hill Top Farm

Warning! Swimming is not allowed in the lake

Esthwaite Water

0·0

1·0

← Esthwaite Lodge

Esthwaite Lodge

Near Sawrey

Windermere Ferry

Hill Top

Trout fishery

P

JCM 10·02·17

O.S. Grid Ref: SD 361 964
Dimensions: 2·5 × 0·6 Km
Max Depth: 24·5 m
Altitude: 66·0m

Beatrix Potter bequeathed 4,000 acres of land & properties to the National Trust in 1943.

ESTHWAITE WATER (17/17)

Saturday 29 October 2016

Today, I am attempting to "tick off" Esthwaite Water, the last lake of my lake challenge. It has proved a hard though extremely successful season of swimming and I am pleased to be finally "hanging up my trunks" for the year.

Not that I can actually go for a dip today. Esthwaite Water is a small lake, 1.5 miles long and 0.5 miles wide, and is a leased as a fishery from the owners, Graythwaite Estate. Unfortunately, the lease agreement with the fishery does not allow swimming, which is most disappointing.

The lake nestles into a timeless enclave of ancient broadleaf woodland and tumbling sheep pasture "the other side" of Windermere. Chilling cloud hovers low, obscuring familiar wooded rises, as I park beside the Fishery buildings, located on the south west shore of the lake (OS Grid Ref: SD361954).

There is an autumnal melancholy about the setting. Lines of ancient beech, with burnished leaves a-tumbling, shield silent, tranquil waters. A few early morning boats float by, their occupants pre-occupied with rod and line.

I chat to a passing fisherman, who is intrigued with my challenge. He tells me that a colleague has already caught two pike this morning; which is not really surprising when you learn that the lake is infamous in angling circles for netting the largest pike ever caught in UK inland waters. This weighed in at a whopping 46.5 lbs!

I head northwards to Hawkshead. Very little of the shore is accessible to the general public and I must walk a network of narrow and sharply winding country lanes to complete a circuit of the lake. It may be reassuring to know that the lake supports a rich and well documented array of flora and fauna as well as being the preserve of the occasional osprey and otter, but it is very frustrating to be kept at least one sheep's pasture distance from so much of the western lake shore.

At long last a muddy path leading from Waterside offers a brief sojourn to a reed fringed shoreline at the northern end of the lake between Waterside Farm and the Nabs. A profound and all-pervading silence is suddenly broken by the percussive roar of a fell farmer ordering his dogs to round up his "yows" from a distant slope.

Beatrix Potter (1866–1943), the much loved children's author, artist and conservationist, was closely associated with these tranquil surroundings. In 1892 she was inspired to write that: "...I have often been laughed at for thinking that Esthwaite Water the most beautiful of the Lakes. It really strikes me that some scenery is almost theatrical or ultra-romantic..."

Extensive wetlands nearly stretch all the way to Hawkshead, lying at the head of the lake. I take the opportunity to visit Beatrix Potter's gallery set in a charming ancient building of low beamed ceilings and rickety timber staircases set in in the heart of village.

Walls are crammed with original artwork from her children's books; lines are drawn so finely and illustrated with exquisitely delicate water colour. As well as the inevitable paintings of Peter Rabbit and Mrs. Tiggy-Winkle, I'm drawn to the images of the frog, Jeremy Fisher, who "...pushes his boat out across Esthwaite Water..."!

I complete my circuit of the lake by following the so called Ferry Road alongside the eastern side of the lake to the tiny hamlet of Near Sawrey. Idyllic it may sound but, rest assured, I hardly expected this segment to prove to be possibly the most dangerous part of my entire Lakeland challenge, considering the absence of any footpaths and foolhardiness of speeding motorists....

My destination is "Hill Top", Beatrix Potter's extraordinary spiritual home. It now serves as a place of pilgrimage for people from the world over.

Beatrix Potter bought Hill Top in 1905 with royalties from her "little white books" and it quickly became a private place of inspiration in which she wrote her stories, painted and lived a simple and happy life. I wander the tiny, quaintly furnished rooms of this darkened house fascinated; it remains a celebration of her life and is filled with her beloved treasures and favourite heirlooms.

Following the phenomenal successes of her children's stories, Beatrix Potter devoted the rest of her life to preserving the Lake District by acquiring and managing a huge estate of farms and land; supporting traditional farming methods; and invigorating the failing stock of indigenous Herdwick sheep.

A final lakeside stroll leads me back to the Fishery car park. Of course, I'm enchanted by this lake and associations. But here is the rub: that Beatrix Potter's favourite lake should remain in private hands and access is denied to nearly all but fee paying anglers. It does not seem right.

Beatrix Potter bequeathed an astonishing 4,000 acres of Lake District to the National Trust on her death in 1943; it still forms the bulk of their holding which comprises a significant 21% chunk of the Lake District National Park.

It is regrettable that the National Trust's stance of caring for the landscape, "for ever, for everyone" is by no means commonplace. The writer and journalist Cal Flyn reported in the September 2014 edition of the "Cumbria Living" Magazine that an estimated 60% of the land in the Lake District National Park is held in private hands. And it is a sobering fact of life that some owners may be indifferent to the beauty of the area, let alone allowing public access across their land.

Fashions come and go; and there is even talk in some quarters of landowners ridding their tenants' sheep from centuries old "hefts" and "re-wilding" the land. It begs a question: how many of us really know or understand the scale and number of perils that might befall this precious and fragile land in the coming years?

FINAL THOUGHTS

Although I never intentionally set out on my swimming challenge to break any records, I am very proud of what I have achieved. Nevertheless, the challenge proved much more arduous and involved than I could ever have dared imagine and it was vital that I never said no, even when the difficulties and restrictions seemed almost insurmountable.

I wrote earlier that I decided to write an account of my journey for four reasons: to celebrate all the good people I have met and marvellous adventures that I have undertaken; to highlight the beauty and fragility of this wonderful land; to draw attention to some failings in water quality, pollution and wanton vandalism I have encountered; and to encourage other swimmers to try swimming in the lakes.

Of course, I will be delighted if my guide goes some small way to inspiring other swimmers to "have a go", but I have to state that my project would never even have got off the ground had it not been for the kindness and generosity of so many people who gave their time and knowledge so freely. It has been an honour to receive such friendship and goodwill.

My challenge has been remarkable for other reasons; it has given me an insight into the rare beauty and also, sadly, the all too obvious fragility of the Lake District. I certainly don't want to come over as a harbinger of doom but I am shocked by the variations in water quality across the lakes.

Admittedly the LDNPA and other organisations are trying, desperately, to improve matters but I do feel that we swimmers have a duty to "Check Clean and Dry" our equipment before and after every swim to restrict the potential damage from non-native invasive species. We also need to report any issues to the authorities to ensure that the lakes gain their necessary protection.

I have been very fortunate to see and experience the Lake District in many of its majestic moods and glories. This privilege is not without its responsibility; I have also witnessed Storm Desmond in the winter of 2015/16 and the ensuing damage and chaos to far too many lakeland communities; the effect will last for years to come.

I can only admire and respect how so many Cumbrians have endured and emerged from the chaos; they are a truly resilient people.

READER'S NOTES

READER'S NOTES

READER'S NOTES

READER'S NOTES

Loweswater swimmers. From left, Tom Baker, John Mather, Paul Ryan and James Slater

Swimming Loweswater in near perfect conditions

Brothers Water. From left, Ben Purdham,
Adam Crawford, Tom Baker, John Mather &
Jordan Hull

Swimming Wast Water in the
shadow of the Screes

Row boat on
Ennerdale
Water

Derwent Water.
Competitors
preparing for the
"Epic Events" one
mile swim

Andy Sims providing valuable support on Wast Water

Starting the
Ullswater
swim,
Glenridding

Resting after the Ullswater
swim. From left, Laura, John
and Robbie Mather